INSTITUTE OF PSYCHIATRY
Maudsley Monographs

MEDICAL REMANDS IN THE CRIMINAL COURT

INSTITUTE OF PSYCHIATRY

MAUDSLEY MONOGRAPHS

Number Twenty-Five

MEDICAL REMANDS IN THE CRIMINAL COURT

By

T. C. N. GIBBENS

M.A., M.D., F.R.C.P., F.R.C.PSYCH.

Professor of Forensic Psychiatry, University of London,
Hon. Consultant Psychiatrist, The Bethlem Royal and The Maudsley Hospital

K. L. SOOTHILL

B.A., PH.D.

Lecturer in Sociology, University of Lancaster
Formerly Research Worker, Institute of Psychiatry

P. J. POPE

B.SC., M.A.

Senior Research Officer, Mid-Glamorgan Social Services Department
Formerly Research Worker, Institute of Psychiatry

OXFORD UNIVERSITY PRESS

1977

Oxford University Press, Walton Street, Oxford OX2 6DP

OXFORD LONDON GLASGOW NEW YORK
TORONTO MELBOURNE WELLINGTON CAPE TOWN
IBADAN NAIROBI DAR ES SALAAM LUSAKA ADDIS ABABA
KUALA LUMPUR SINGAPORE JAKARTA HONG KONG TOKYO
DELHI BOMBAY CALCUTTA MADRAS KARACHI

© *Institute of Psychiatry 1977*

British Library Cataloguing in Publication Data

Gibbens, Trevor Charles Noel
  Medical remands in the criminal court.
  – (Maudsley monographs; 25).
  1. Criminal procedure – England 2. Police
  magistrates – England
  I. Title II. Soothill, Keith III. Pope,
  Patrick IV. Institute of Psychiatry V. Series
  345'.42'077   KD8309

ISBN 0-19-712147-0

Printed in Great Britain
by Richard Clay (The Chaucer Press), Ltd,
Bungay, Suffolk

CONTENTS

LIST OF APPENDICES

1. The use of charge sheets as a documentary source in the Study of Medical Remands
2. Questionnaire completed by hospital consultants and prison medical officers
3. Total time from first court appearance to date of sentence for Inner London (1969) sample
4. Number and proportion of Inner London (1969) sample held in custody throughout court process
5. Comparison of Inner London and Wessex areas in terms of the sentence of the court (1969) samples
6. Present mental state of Wessex (1970–1) sample (Ratings of the psychiatrists to each of five items)
7. Basic personality or life-style of Wessex (1970–1) sample (Ratings of the psychiatrists to each of four items)
8. Relationship between Mental Health Assessment and court sentence

MAUDSLEY MONOGRAPHS

HENRY MAUDSLEY, from whom the series of monographs takes its name, was the founder of The Maudsley Hospital and the most prominent English psychiatrist of his generation. The Maudsley Hospital was united with the Bethlem Royal Hospital in 1948, and its medical school, renamed the Institute of Psychiatry at the same time, became a constituent part of the British Postgraduate Medical Federation. It is entrusted by the University of London with the duty to advance psychiatry by teaching and research.

The monograph series reports work carried out in the Institute and in the associated Hospital. Some of the monographs are directly concerned with clinical problems; others, less obviously relevant, are in scientific fields that are cultivated for the furtherance of psychiatry.

Joint Editors

PROFESSOR SIR DENIS HILL
F.R.C.P., F.R.C.PSYCH., D.P.M.

PROFESSOR G. S. BRINDLEY
M.D., F.R.C.P., F.R.S.

with the assistance of

MISS S. E. HAGUE, B.SC. (ECON.), M.A.

ACKNOWLEDGEMENTS

WE wish to express our appreciation of the support given to this study by the Home Office through their Research Fund and for their permission to publish this report; publication does not imply that they share the views expressed. Some of the material in Chapters 3 and 4 has already been published in a shortened version as an ISTD booklet (Medical Remands in Magistrates' Courts, 1974) and we are grateful for permission to re-present in a modified form. We are also indebted to Mrs. A. Stevens for her help with the high court study and to Miss K. Coomes and Mrs. M. Bartholomew for secretarial work.

Much of this study involved obtaining information which exists in different forms in different places and we would not have succeeded without the most willing co-operation of many individuals and organizations. In particular, we must mention the records division of New Scotland Yard and the City of London police, and the Criminal Records office; the Clerks of all the courts, and all the consultant psychiatrists and probation officers in Wessex; the Wessex Regional Hospital Board; the prison medical officers and hospital officers; the assistance of the Home Office Statistical Division and the advice of the Home Office Research Unit were also invaluable. Finally, we are grateful to the editors of the Monograph series and especially to Miss Hague for their painstaking revision of the text. To them all we offer our warmest thanks.

T. C. N. GIBBENS
K. L. SOOTHILL
P. J. POPE

CHAPTER I

INTRODUCTION

THIS study, planned as the first of a series on medical aspects of the prison medical service, supported by grants from the Home Office, was stimulated by the observation that increasing numbers of offenders are remanded in *custody* by the magistrates' courts for medical (mainly psychiatric) reports before conviction or sentence, although prisons, especially local prisons or remand centres (for those aged 17–21) where such reports are prepared, are overcrowded and prison medical officers are under pressure. Apart from the expense the most serious question is whether sentencing minor offenders to what amounts to three weeks' imprisonment is just or desirable when the aim of penal policy is to reduce prison sentences. As early as 1923, the prison commissioners had commented in respect of custodial remands on 'the stigma of committal to prison and the danger of becoming known by sight to old offenders'.[1] We shall see later that in 1967 (Dell and Gibbens, 1971) out of many hundreds of women remanded to Holloway prison, less than 9 per cent received a 'hospital order' and not more than another 10 per cent were sentenced to imprisonment or Borstal training. Thus 80 per cent of the women sent to prison for medical examination were released in the community after the remand period, perhaps because they had already been three weeks in custody. The magistrates had probably never intended to do other than fine, discharge absolutely or conditionally or place on probation, unless doctors recommended differently.

This is part of the problem of communication between magistrates, administration, and doctors. The magistrates, who are seldom medically qualified, have to decide when a medical report would be helpful, often with no information except what has transpired in court; the administration has to arrange for reports as often and as soon as required, and the doctors have to decide what, if any, treatment to recommend. We accordingly have tried to examine, in the light of contemporary practice, several basic questions: what proportion of offenders is remanded for a medical report, and how many receive custody or bail for the purpose? Are some types of offender remanded for medical reports more often that others? What decisions do the courts make in consequence, and does this differ for those given custody or bail? Are there significant regional variations in practice?

The numbers remanded in *custody* for medical reports are given in the annual reports of the Prison Department. TABLE I shows their rate of increase since 1961 (by over 30 per cent since 1965).

[1] Report of the Commissioners of Prisons 1923–24. Cmnd. 2307, p. 12.

However, the number of offenders coming before the courts has also steadily increased, and there is no evidence that the *proportion* of offenders remanded for medical examination has increased significantly. The number of offenders coming before magistrates' courts (and either sentenced or committed to a higher court for trial or sentence) has also increased (by 28 per cent). The magistrates themselves dispose of the majority of offenders; the proportion is now 98 per cent. The present study is primarily concerned with medical reports to the magistrates' courts, with whom the bulk of decisions lie. Medical reports to higher courts are examined in less detail separately. Although numerically small, they are important in relation to the sentencing of major offenders.

TABLE 1

REMANDS IN CUSTODY FOR MEDICAL REPORTS 1961–1975[1]

	Remands for Medical Reports	% Change over Previous Year
1961	6,366	—
1962	7,015	+10·2
1963	7,881	+12·3
1964	7,782	− 1·3
1965	9,555	+22·8
1966	10,919	+14·3
1967	11,061	+ 1·3
1968	11,846	+ 7·1
1969	13,452	+13·6
1970	13,680	+ 1·7
1971	12,969	− 5·2
1972	11,953	− 7·8
1973	12,542	+ 4·9
1974	12,530	− 0·1
1975	11,912	− 4·9

N.B.   These figures refer to reports for magistrates' *and* high courts.

TABLE 1 refers only to medical reports prepared in *custody*. No official information exists about reports prepared during bail, and a major task was to find out how, within the limits of time and resources, we could obtain this information, whether the majority of medical reports on bail are prepared by N.H.S. psychiatrists or private doctors and whether the recent slowing down of the rate of increase in the number of reports prepared in custody by the Prison Medical Service is due to increased use of reports on bail.

Few previous studies have specifically examined the problems of remand for medical reports. West and Bearcroft (1960) compared a sample of offenders remanded in custody for medical reports at Brixton prison with a sample seen on bail at the Maudsley hospital and Portman clinic. They expected custody to be related to the dangerousness of the offence, previous convictions, previous imprisonment, excessive drinking, being unemployed, or not having a settled address. Though the distribution of offences differed

[1] *Reports on the Work of the Prison Department 1961–75*, H.M.S.O.

considerably in the two samples, sexual offenders forming a much higher proportion of those referred to outside clinics and property and aggressive offenders predominating in the custody sample, a very considerable overlap in type of social background was found in both samples when they were equated for type of crime. The authors concluded that if the expected criteria had been adhered to, remands in custody would have been reduced by one-third; and if only dangerous offenders or those of no fixed abode had been remanded in custody the number would have fallen by two-thirds.

Sparks (1966) examined remands for medical reports in 1961 in two central London courts served by stipendiary magistrates. One court remanded 329 cases and the other 165, i.e. 2·9 per cent and 2·5 per cent of the cases heard. All but one were remanded in custody and only four were remanded before trial. The study demonstrated a great variation between courts in the number of mentally abnormal cases appearing before them. The first court accounted for almost one-third of the hospital orders made in the Metropolitan Magistrates' Courts during 1961 and over a quarter of the total made by all magistrates' courts in the whole of the Metropolitan Police District.

The Home Office Research Unit (Gibson, 1960) studied time spent awaiting trial by magistrates' and high courts in 1958. Of those dealt with only by the magistrates' courts 7 per cent were remanded for reports and 29 per cent for other reasons. The two groups overlapped, for about a third of the group remanded for reports (medical, probation, or suitability for Borstal) had also been remanded for other reasons: the total proportion remanded before trial was 31 per cent and the proportion remanded on bail was 64 per cent. In respect of remands for specific reports the latter proportion was exactly reversed, 64 per cent being remanded in custody.

Scott (1967) asked magistrates at one court to list their reasons for remanding juveniles in custody for a psychiatric report. In addition to the usual reasons—seriousness of the offence, no fixed abode, danger to self, and others, etc.—other 'hidden' reasons were admitted in a quarter to a third; 'as a form of warning' was included in 25 per cent.

Dell and Gibbens (1971) examined one in four of all admissions of women and girls to Holloway prison in 1967. Of women remanded in custody 56 per cent were for medical reports. Of these less than 9 per cent received compulsory hospital admissions (Section 60 and 65 Mental Health Act, 1959) and less than 10 per cent received a subsequent sentence of imprisonment or Borstal training; thus 80 per cent of these women were set free after return to court. Suitability for bail was assessed by criteria developed experimentally by the Vera Institute of New York in the Manhattan Bail Project, points being given for factors in the social background which militated against non-appearance at court when bailed. We also made a more rigorous individual assessment; on the Vera system 34 per cent were classed as suitable for bail; on individual assessment 39 per cent.

Many recent studies of bail have pointed out its relationship to the granting of legal aid (Dell, 1971) and other factors (Bottomley, 1970): unless they are legally aided, offenders may not know they are entitled to bail or what bail is. However, it is often difficult to extract the motive of remand for medical reports in such studies. There is also evidence that the situation is complicated by both personal factors (the attitude, expectations and motives of magistrates) and problems of where and how to obtain a report, and how to interpret it.

PROCEDURES FOR DEALING WITH THE ABNORMAL OFFENDER

At this stage it may be helpful to give the non-legal reader an account of the steps that can be taken by police and courts in dealing with offenders, noting those procedures which apply especially to the abnormal offender. The law is complex and detailed but what follows should be adequate.

1. The police may caution or advise a person who commits a minor offence or breach of the peace. As far as we know no studies of this aspect of police discretion have been made in this country in relation to mentally abnormal offenders, but an observational study has been made in the U.S.A. (Bittner, 1967) of police attitudes to mental illness and mental abnormality. The police in England and Wales are extremely tolerant of mentally abnormal persons who do not present a threat to themselves or others, though they may cause the police considerable nuisance by raising false alarms, complaining of persecution or making false confessions to major crimes, etc.

2. The commonest police procedure to deal with mentally disordered persons who have caused or are likely to cause a breach of the peace is to call in a mental welfare officer, who makes arrangements with the doctor for admission to hospital either voluntarily or under Section 29 (72 hour order) or Section 28 (28 day order) of the Mental Health Act of 1959.

3. The Mental Health Act gives special powers to the police in mentally abnormal cases. Section 136 provides that 'if a constable finds *in a place to which the public have access* a person who appears to him to be suffering from mental disorder and to be in immediate need of care and control, the constable may if he thinks it necessary to do so in the interests of that person, or for the protection of other persons, remove that person to a place of safety'—in practice a mental ward or hospital. The patient may be detained for 72 hours.

The use of Section 136 was studied by George (1972). It varied considerably: 21 of the 32 police forces called in the mental welfare officer to deal with the problem, only four forces used Section 136 in most cases. Of these, by far the most important were the Metropolitan Police who were alone responsible for 80 per cent of all such admissions. Only one force always called a police surgeon. The only police authority which closely resembled that of the Metropolitan Police was the Northumberland force where

Section 136 cases amounted to a third (34 per cent) of emergency compulsory orders (Sections 29, 25, and 136) in 1969.

By 1969 the numbers of admissions had increased to 1,429 in England and Wales, and 1,169 in the metropolitan area. Nearly half (48 per cent) of Section 136 admissions occurred in the South West Metropolitan Regional Hospital Board area and amounted to 17 per cent of all emergency compulsory admissions (i.e. Sections 29, 25, and 136). The great majority of arrests occurred in the boroughs of Westminster, Kensington and Chelsea, and Hammersmith; some peripheral boroughs had only one per cent of such arrests.

Those dealt with in this way tended to have caused public disturbance by threatening or bizarre behaviour: wandering, self neglect (28 per cent), suicidal attempts or threats (8 per cent), verbal and physical aggression (24 per cent), expression of gross delusions (14 per cent), sexual misbehaviour (9 per cent), confusion (8 per cent), 'apparent crime' (3 per cent), traffic disturbances (5 per cent), etc. George shows that those dealt with under Section 136 differed from those admitted compulsorily by mental welfare officers under Section 29 (72 hour orders): the police admissions had significantly more often shown aggressive behaviour before admission (42 per cent compared with 21 per cent), continued to show aggressive or uncooperative behaviour after admission (63 per cent compared with 43 per cent), were more often of no fixed abode (26 per cent; 7 per cent) and had been previously admitted under the same Section 136 (29 per cent against 6 per cent of Section 29 cases; 55 per cent of the latter had however been previously admitted under Section 29). To some extent, therefore, they might have been known to the police already and might even have been locally well-known characters. Females were well represented (42 per cent) and their disturbed behaviour had similar characteristics, in similar proportions. In London the diagnosis has to be made by a policeman of inspector's rank, and mistakes were rare; only one per cent or less were thought to show no mental abnormality after admission, and over half suffered from schizophrenia.[1]

Although there is clearly a difference between Section 136 and Section 29 cases in London, depending upon which agency acts first, it is not clear whether throughout the country the same type of mentally disordered person (manifestly disturbed in public and not having committed any serious offence) is dealt with similarly by the one or other method, and not charged or taken to court.

A patient admitted under Section 136 may occasionally be charged subsequently with an offence, either as a result of later information or if his

[1] Many hospitals will not admit patients under Section 136 (this no doubt is known to the local police). If a well-known psychotic behaves in a way which has to be controlled (e.g. in one case, chasing small girls in a jocular and harmless way which nevertheless frightened them) and the hospital will not admit (or more often re-admit) him, he may be brought to court to be 'bound over to keep the peace' without a specific charge, under a medieval but convenient act.

behaviour is considered to have been dangerous enough (e.g. brandishing a knife) to make a court order for hospital detention desirable, rather than a decision by the doctors alone.

4. If a policeman knows of an offence and the identity of the offender, he may apply to a magistrate for a *summons* requiring the offender to appear before a court on a certain date. In other cases he applies for a warrant; or if he catches the offender 'in the act', he will arrest him and, unless the offence is trivial and can be ignored or dealt with by a caution, charge him.

If the police decide to take the individual into custody, section 38 (4) of the Magistrates' Courts Act 1952 requires a person retained in custody to be brought before a court 'as soon as practicable'. A court appearance is normally within 24 hours, but section 38 (1) in fact requires that, if it is not practicable to bring the person before a court within the 24 hours, the police must consider the question of bail and, unless the offence appears serious, release him on bail.

Our research follows on from the stage when the person is actually charged and a charge sheet is made out. After charging the individual the police decide whether to release him at once on 'police bail', with or without 'recognizances' of a sum of money promised by the offender and/or his friends, or to keep him in police custody until the court appearance. The abnormal offender may be sent home at this stage if he has relatives to look after him, but the homeless, the acutely disturbed, or the potential dangers will tend to be kept in police custody until the court can review the case. The decision, however, is an extremely practical one, made with a knowledge of many of the circumstances.

After the magistrates have heard the case and are satisfied of the accused's guilt, if the accused is suspected of being abnormal he may be remanded to prison or on bail for a medical report under Section 26 of the Magistrates' Courts Act, 1952 ('if . . . the court is satisfied the offence has been committed by the accused, but is of opinion that an enquiry ought to be made into his physical or mental condition . . . the court shall adjourn the case to enable a medical examination and report to be made'): the accused, however, can be remanded to prison for a medical report under this Section only if the alleged offence is one for which he could be sent to prison if convicted. The procedure of remanding prior to recording a conviction is especially important, however, because if the medical report indicates that the person is mentally ill or severely subnormal (but not if he is suffering from the other two categories of disorder—psychopathic disorder or subnormality) the court may order detention in hospital (Section 60) *without recording a conviction*. This can be important, for some jobs are barred, and some foreign countries refuse visas, to those who have had a criminal conviction.

Apart from their powers under Section 26, magistrates also have the power under Section 14 (3) of the Magistrates' Court Act, 1952[1] to remand a

---

[1] The Criminal Justice Act of 1967 made an important distinction between Section 14 (3) and Section 26 cases. The new Act limits the remand in custody for those under Section 14

convicted offender for inquiries (medical or otherwise) whether or not the offence is imprisonable. Such remands can be in custody or on bail and in fact the great majority of medical remands in custody are under this section.

There are many reasons for remanding, either on bail or in custody; e.g. if it is alleged that he has dangerous drugs in his possession, these may have to be chemically analysed, the police need time for further inquiries, or the defence apply for time to prepare their defence, including if they wish a medical report on his state of mind. Remands for a social inquiry by a probation officer alone are much more frequent than remands for medical reports, though the latter are often accompanied by a request for a probation report as well. In Dell and Gibbens' study (1971) of 638 women received into Holloway prison, there were the following multi-purpose remands at various stages (the figures in brackets show the number who received a custodial sentence to prison or Borstal after return to court):

Magistrates' courts' remands for medical inquiries	168 (13)
Pre-trial remands with simultaneous requests for medical report	10 (3)
Committal for sentence to a higher court with simultaneous request for medical report	6 (3)
Request for report upon suitability for Borstal (by the governor) as well as medical report	12 (1)
Judgement respited with request for medical report	6 (1)
Magistrates remand for medical report, preceded by pre-trial remand in custody	33 (3)

5. When the offender returns to court with his medical report the magistrates can take three main courses of action if medical treatment is recommended.

(a) If the accused is so ill or confused as to be 'unfit to plead' (i.e. cannot follow the proceedings, cannot distinguish a plea of guilty from not guilty, is unable to instruct counsel for his defence, etc.),[1] the magistrates cannot under present law find him unfit to plead but must commit him to a higher court, where a jury can find him unfit to plead. However, if the offence is relatively trivial the police may either withdraw the charge, or the magistrates may dismiss the case, in the knowledge that two doctors have signed a civil commitment order under Section 25 of the Mental Health Act for detention in a mental hospital for 28 days.

(with certain important exceptions for those who have served a previous prison sentence, have ever skipped bail, have no fixed address, or have committed a crime of violence, etc.); but Section 18 of the Act says that the limitation on power of remand in custody 'shall not apply to the adjournment for trial by a magistrates' court under Section 26 for the purposes of enabling a medical examination and report to be made on the offender *if it appears to the court that it would be impracticable to obtain such a report without remanding the defendant in custody*'.

[1] The Criminal Administration Act of 1967 merely says 'is under disability in conducting his defence' but since this may be said of a wide range of accused, the old criteria tend to persist.

Such offenders are similar to those admitted to hospital direct by the police under Section 136, with the difference that a definite offence has been committed, even though minor and not necessarily in a public place. This use of Section 25, however, is relatively uncommon.

(b) The magistrates can make a probation order on condition that the offender receives in-patient or out-patient treatment (Section 4, Criminal Justice Act, 1948). A doctor must sign the recommendation and he or another doctor must agree to undertake the treatment. If the remand is in custody the prison medical officer must obtain the agreement of an outside consultant to undertake the treatment. We shall call this for the sake of brevity 'a psychiatric probation order'. The procedure is designed for those who will voluntarily accept treatment, and since they are free to leave hospital or treatment at any time (even though it could involve a breach of probation) it is used for those who do not present a serious danger to the public.

(c) On the recommendation of two doctors, one of whom must be recognized by the local authority as experienced in the diagnosis of mental disorder, the magistrates may commit the offender to a mental hospital with or without his consent (Section 60 of the Mental Health Act). This is the so-called 'hospital order'. He is then liable to arrest if he absconds or leaves without the responsible doctor's consent.

The magistrates have no power to make a 'restriction order' (i.e. an order under Section 65 of the Mental Health Act by which the offender is committed to hospital with restriction of discharge for a specified or unlimited time unless the Secretary of State consents to his release). The magistrates can, however, commit him to a higher court with a view to such order. The responsible doctor cannot thereafter release or transfer the patient during the specified period without consent from the Home Office.

Our task was to study how these procedures were used, within the general framework of operation of the courts, by which the magistrates decide that they need a medical report, where they are to obtain one, and what to do when they have received it.

CHAPTER II

THE METHOD OF STUDY

INFORMATION on three topics was needed:

(1) The numbers of medical reports requested, at what stage in the proceedings this occurred, whether the report was obtained in custody or on bail, and the outcome.

(2) 'The turnover' of each court, i.e. how many offenders by age, sex and type of offence came before it. This was to throw light on the selection of cases and the frequency with which reports were requested.

(3) Clinical psychiatric information about the cases which the psychiatrist examined, how the psychiatrists saw their role, and what recommendations they made.

This proved much more difficult to obtain than had been expected. It seemed unavoidable that we should study the situation in London whose courts deal with a quarter of all indictable offences in England and Wales. Brixton prison alone provides about one-third of all the psychiatric reports in the country which are made in custody—some 4,000 out of 13,000 reports, but a detailed study of London practice was impossible with the resources available. The type of offender coming before the courts varies considerably so that a wide range of courts would have had to be included. It would be difficult to find out where cases remanded on bail had been examined and by whom. London was then divided very irregularly into four metropolitan regional hospital board areas—North East, North West, South West, South East—reaching in segments into the centre but broadening out into the suburbs and country. Some central courts which deal with a high proportion of mentally abnormal offenders were concentrated within the south western region. Although the hospital board areas might be adhered to for those seen in custody (in practice they are not), this could not apply to bail cases. It would be absurd for a court within one hospital board area not to make use of a clinic or hospital a few streets away in another regional hospital board area. In London the areas served by hospital boards, police divisions, and magistrates' courts do not correspond.

The situation in London would, it was expected, differ from that elsewhere so we had to combine a study of London with one of a regional hospital board area away from London in which the drainage areas of health services, prison, magistrates' courts and police divisions corresponded or could be adjusted to correspond with considerable accuracy.

The Wessex Regional Hospital Board area proved very suitable. Thirty-eight magistrates' courts corresponded with the Regional Board's area; Wessex psychiatrists saw all cases for reports on bail. Those remanded in custody were all detained in Winchester prison or remand centre, except for an identifiable proportion in the rest of the region who were remanded to Dorchester prison. Moreover the forty consultant psychiatrists and medical officers in the hospital board area, Winchester and Dorchester prisons, could all be visited to discuss the purposes of the study and invite their co-operation. The Board moreover had a reputation for being co-operative and understanding about the needs of research. We were extremely grateful for the co-operation of all concerned.

A pilot study of feasibility of numbers, facilities, and documentation was then necessary.

THE PILOT INQUIRIES

All medical reports on males[1] supplied by Brixton prison and Ashford Remand Centre (which was for men 17–21) during the three-month period 1 October–31 December 1969 were listed: 712 were from Brixton and 419 from Ashford. Although reports from Brixton were made to 71 different magistrates' courts in the Home Counties, 60 per cent were supplied to only ten central London courts, and 57 per cent of the reports from Ashford to eleven central courts. Although at that time the total numbers appearing before these particular courts were not known, there was no doubt where the main demand was coming from, and this determined which courts should be studied. The number of courts was brought up to eighteen, including the City of London, to make a single central London area in which the courts requested about a quarter of all such reports in England and Wales.

In Wessex 110 medical reports had been supplied to the courts in the hospital board area[2] (88 from Winchester prison, 22 from Dorchester prison); 49 per cent of these reports to magistrates' courts had been supplied to only three courts. This relatively small total number led us to hope that later we might be able to carry out a detailed clinical study of all cases in the board's area.

Perhaps a more serious problem concerned which cases appearing before a court had been remanded for a medical report and at what stage. The court registers include a daily record of cases seen, but not the progress of a particular individual nor always the reason for a remand. To get information from all the London consultants or clinics that might have been involved was out of the question.

The police charge sheets were the best source of information for the

[1] The pilot study was concerned exclusively with male offenders. Females who are custodially remanded in London are sent to Holloway prison, while females in Wessex have to go to Holloway in London or Pucklechurch near Bristol.

[2] We later discovered that a few young offenders also went to Exeter remand centre and we considered these in the main study.

Metropolitan Police area. They recorded both basic information about the individual offender and his progress through the courts, including whether a remand (of any kind) was made and the place and conditions of the remand. For 16 of the courts, 117,000 sheets from 14 police divisions had to be sorted, to locate the medical remands but the search for the two City of London courts was a much less onerous task. We are extremely grateful to the Metropolitan Police and the City of London Police for allowing access to the records.

In Wessex the charge sheets unfortunately could not be used for tracing medical remands, for in one large police force the purpose of the remand was not included and the court registers of all 38 courts in the area had to be checked for 1969. This was laborious for not all the purposes of remand were given and in doubtful cases the individual records of the proceedings had to be examined.

The court registers moreover covered more individuals than those to whom the charge sheets alone related.[1] In the metropolitan area a few medical remands had probably been lost, and in Wessex some medical remands for 'summonsed' cases might have been included.

The retrospective study (i.e. based upon past records) was accordingly planned to compare all medical remands of those convicted in 1969 in eighteen Inner London courts, and in all the courts in the Wessex Regional Hospital Board area, with total numbers by age, sex, offence, and sentence of all offenders coming before these courts. This yielded the following numbers:

TABLE 2
MEDICAL REMANDS

	Males	Females	Total
Inner London	3,310	650	3,960
Wessex	413	77	490
Total	3,723	727	4,450

After the survey of the magistrates' courts a supplementary comparison on the same year was carried out of remands for medical reports by the higher courts, and by quarter sessions or assizes dealing with those who had passed through the selected magistrates' courts (18 in Inner London, 38 in Wessex). The higher courts were the Inner London Quarter Sessions and the Central Criminal Court (the Old Bailey), and 12 courts in the Wessex Regional Hospital Board area, namely, the Quarter Sessions of Hampshire, Winchester City, Andover, Portsmouth, and Southampton, Isle of Wight, Bournemouth, Poole and Dorset, and the Assize courts of Hampshire, Dorset, and Wiltshire.

[1] APPENDIX I gives a fuller description of charge sheets and a discussion of their use compared with the summons.

The main source of information for the Wessex higher courts on persons remanded for a medical report was contained in post-trial calendars. These calendars had the same sort of information as court registers but with the valuable addition of previous convictions. For London higher courts post-trial calendars were not available, so court registers were used. However, for the three London higher courts in the sample there were some pre-trial calendars of court proceedings, but previous conviction data were available systematically only for persons dealt with by these courts in 1969 and early 1970.

Since the passage of the Courts Act 1971 there has been the full scale introduction of Crown Courts in place of the old divisions of Assize Courts and Courts of Quarter Sessions, but this has probably not had a very great effect upon the procedures of medical remands. As Borrie (1971) reminds us: 'no one should imagine that a revolution has occurred in our judicial system just because such deep established institutions as Assizes and Quarter Sessions have been abolished'.

THE PROSPECTIVE STUDY

The retrospective study provided reliable statistical information but was limited mainly to age, sex, type of offence, and type of sentence. The relatively small number involved in Wessex encouraged a more detailed study in this area.

Accordingly during 1970, while the 1969 sample was being collected, all 40 consultant psychiatrists and prison medical officers in the region were visited. Their attitude to experience of forensic cases was discussed; they were asked to estimate how many cases from the courts they had seen in the last year, to record any cases referred to them from September 1970 'until further notice', and to fill in a questionnaire about social and psychiatric aspects of offenders who would be referred.

The drafting of this questionnaire (see APPENDIX 2) had difficulties. Though the main categories of mental illness are well defined, there is no acceptable classification of personality disorders and doctors' interpretation of the questions would vary. We sent a pilot questionnaire to the doctors working in Brixton prison and noted their comments and criticisms. In addition to clinical data, the questionnaire included questions about preparation of reports, machinery of referral, etc. Medical reports and questionnaires were collected for eight months—from 1 September 1970 to 30 April 1971. Court records were checked to make sure that no medical remands were missed. Information was also sought from the probation service, and many officers at the principal courts co-operated in interviews. In Wessex virtually all offenders are interviewed before trial or before sentence. We asked probation officers to fill in questionnaires dealing with social information about those remanded for medical reports, and, to obtain a control group by which to compare those medically remanded with those who were not, also to supply the report which they prepared on the 'next case' of the same sex for whom they were asked to prepare a social inquiry report. This, though restricted to males, proved over-ambitious: probation reports may be prepared long after or before the medical remand and there was also a postal strike at the critical stage. TABLE 3 shows how many questionnaires were completed.

TABLE 3
QUESTIONNAIRES COMPLETED

Source of Data	Males	% Possible Returns	Females	Returns % Possible
Magistrates' Courts Sample	287	100	56	100
Medical Officers (Prison and Hospital)	256	89·2	43	76·8
Probation Officers' Reports (Medical Cases)	130*	45·3	—	—
Probation Officers' Reports (Control cases)	114	39·7	—	—

* For the analysis in CHAPTER VIII, we restricted the discussion to the 114 cases where the probation officer had also suppled a suitable control case.

Other possible sources of medical evidence which might influence the court, or its decision to order a remand were also important. All the consultants were, therefore, asked to fill in a questionnaire (see APPENDIX 2) for any case on which they were requested to report on behalf of the defence, and prison medical officers were similarly asked about voluntary or unsolicited reports submitted. We had no means of checking whether all such examinations were reported to us, but as consultants and prison medical officers were very reliable in the other ways to which they assisted the study, we do not think that there are any serious gaps here.

SUMMARY OF RESEARCH DESIGN

The study, therefore, consisted of

A. *Retrospective Study*. Inner London and Wessex, 1969.

(1) Details by age, sex, type of crime, and type of disposal of all cases remanded for a medical report in the eighteen Inner London courts and thirty-eight Wessex courts throughout 1969. Similar details for the appropriate High Courts in the two areas.

(2) Similar information about the other offenders coming before each of these courts.

B. *Prospective Study*. Wessex 1970–1.

(1) Reports and completed questionnaires about all offenders remanded for a medical report in Wessex only between September 1 1970 and 30 April 1971.

(2) Social inquiry reports on these offenders by probation officers.

(3) Social inquiry reports by probation officers on the next succeeding case of the same sex seen by them during their work, as a control sample.

(4) Reports and completed questionnaires on medical defence reports to Wessex magistrates as well as voluntary or unsolicited reports submitted by prison medical officers.

PART I: RETROSPECTIVE STUDY

CHAPTER III

FREQUENCY OF THE MEDICAL REMAND IN THE MAGISTRATES' COURTS

CONTRARY to popular belief, the presentation of medical evidence is unusual in the court process and occurs only in a few criminal cases. Our concern was primarily with the magistrates' courts and the involvement of psychiatrists in the immense amount of work being carried out by these courts.

From the viewpoint of the prison service the courts make a great deal of use of the medical remand. As we have seen in CHAPTER I (see TABLE I, page 2), the number of *custodial* remands has more than doubled in less than ten years. By concentrating on the activities of the magistrates' courts we can consider the source of the greatest potential increase in the pressure on the medical services, such as would happen if courts desired more medical evidence to assist them in their deliberations either on culpability or treatability. For example, if magistrates' courts remanded in custody for a medical report a further 5 per cent of all offenders found guilty of an indictable offence, present demands upon the prison medical resources would double. However, the present position is not clear. Sparks (1966) found that in two London magistrates' courts the rate of remand for medical reports during 1961 was less than 3 per cent of the total cases heard, but it is not known whether the proportion of persons remanded for medical reports by magistrates' courts is the same as when Sparks carried out his work and whether the proportions remanded for a medical report regardless of sex, age, or offence are similar. If in fact they are, this would suggest that magistrates do not systematically relate any of these characteristics to the need for a medical remand, but our findings suggest that magistrates do ask for a higher proportion of medical reports in certain categories. There are various explanations for this and it is relevant to consider how these data relate to the proportion who actually receive a medical disposal after the medical reports have been presented to the courts.

No court turnover figures were supplied for those appearing in court solely for 'breach of probation order', and such medical remands were therefore excluded from the subsequent analysis in this chapter. Nevertheless, magistrates seemed more ready to remand females for a medical report after the apparent failure of a probation order. Whereas only 14 (or 0·4 per cent) of the 3,310 males medically remanded in Inner London and only 6 (or 1·5 per cent) of 413 males so remanded in Wessex were for 'breach of probation order' only, 28 (or 4 per cent) of the Inner London females and 6 (or 7·8 per cent) of the Wessex females were so remanded.

Court Turnover of Indictable Offences

Although the medical remand was comparatively rare in the magistrates' court, the proportion of persons convicted in the lower courts of an *indictable* offence and remanded for a medical report at some state in the court proceedings, was nearly one in ten (TABLE 4). This, as will be shown later, compares with a figure of about one in a hundred among those convicted for non-indictable offences. Non-indictable offences greatly outnumbered indictable offences, so the total proportion of persons remanded for medical reports in the lower courts was probably 2 or 3 per cent of the court turnover.

Sparks (1966) was not able to consider from his material regional differences, if any, in the use of the medical remand. On the assumption that mentally abnormal persons will drift to urban centres, there is likely to be a much higher proportion of persons in the metropolis in respect of whom the magistrates would want a psychiatric report to help them in disposal.

TABLE 4 shows that, for both males and females, the proportion of those committing indictable offences remanded for a medical report was higher in Inner London than in Wessex.

TABLE 4

NUMBER AND PERCENTAGE OF MEDICAL REMANDS IN TERMS OF THE COURT TURNOVER (INDICTABLE OFFENCES ONLY)

	No. of Medical Remands	No. in Court Turnover	% of Medical Remands
Inner London Magistrates' Courts			
Males	2,027	21,909	9·3
Females	377	5,278	7·1
Total	2,404	27,187	8·8
Wessex Magistrates' Courts			
Males	306	7,076	4·3
Females	66	1,194	5·5
Total	372	8,270	4·5

For each age group (17–20; 21–29; 30 and over) the pattern was the same, as TABLE 5 demonstrates, except that for the age group 17–20 Inner London magistrates favoured a medical remands for males, while Wessex magistrates tended to apply it to females. These figures, of course, included young men convicted by magistrates' courts and sent to a higher court for sentencing. Courts, when considering a custodial sentence for a young offender, might have tended to ask for a medical report in addition to reports as to Borstal suitability and 'fitness for detention centre'. In Wessex there was no remand centre for females (females custodially remanded had to go to Holloway in London or Pucklechurch near Bristol) and magistrates might thus have asked for a medical report in marginal cases for young females on the grounds that this would prevent lengthy cases; and they might also have thought a medical remand useful if a custodial remand was deemed necessary for other reasons.

TABLE 5

NUMBER AND PERCENTAGE OF MEDICAL REMANDS IN TERMS OF SEX AND AGE (INDICTABLE OFFENCES ONLY)

	Males			Females		
Age	No. of medical remands	No. in court turnover	% of medical remands	No. of medical remands	No. in court turnover	% of medical remands
Inner London Magistrates' Courts						
17–20	761	5,785	13·2	112	1,281	8·7
21–29	574	8,170	7·0	123	1,766	7·0
30+	692	7,954	8·7	142	2,231	6·4
Total	2,027	21,909	9·2	377	5,278	7·1
Wessex Magistrates' Courts						
17–20	86	2,349	3·7	29	263	11·0
21–29	117	2,590	4·5	18	314	5·7
30+	102	2,137	4·8	18	617	2·9
Total	306*	7,076	4·3	66*	1,194	5·5

* Includes one case for whom the age was unknown.

Except for the difference just mentioned, the two areas showed similar patterns for other categories, though the Inner London rates were higher.

However, TABLE 6 shows a different picture for type of offence. The figure for offences of violence against the person was comparatively low, but this might have been because the more serious violence offences as well as those regarded by magistrates as due to disturbed behaviour were sent for trial by a higher court. The male sexual offender was more frequently selected for a medical remand, whereas for rarer female offences (burglary, fraud, and forgery) the proportion of medical remands was comparatively high. Again, in Wessex, the proportion of medical remands was consistently lower for each indictable offence category considered, except for indictable sexual offenders; in *both* areas magistrates favoured the medical remand for sexual offenders. These figures generally suggest that Wessex magistrates are more selective about their choice of medical remands.

TABLE 6
NUMBER AND PERCENTAGE OF MEDICAL REMANDS IN TERMS OF PRINCIPAL INDICTABLE OFFENCE

Principal Indictable Offence	Males			Females		
	No. of Medical Remands	No. in Court Turnover	% of Medical Remands	No. of Medical Remands	No. in Court Turnover	% of Medical Remands
Inner London Magistrates' Courts						
Violence against the person	114	1,930	5·9	20	224	8·9
Sexual offences	113	589	19·2	—	—	—
Offences against property with violence	383	2,606	14·7	20	64	31·3
Unauthorized taking of motor vehicle	250	2,133	11·7	9	48	18·8
Theft, shoplifting, handling stolen goods	881	12,288	7·2	242	4,392	5·5
Fraud, forgery	268	2,199	12·2	85	515	16·5
Other indictable offences	18	164	11·0	1	35	2·9
Total	2,027	21,909	9·3	377	5,278	7·1
Wessex Magistrates' Courts						
Violence against the person	22	566	3·9	1	16	6·3
Sexual offences	37	178	20·8	0	1	0
Offences against property with violence	81	1,101	7·4	5	32	15·6
Unauthorized taking of motor vehicle	16	672	2·4	0	26	0
Theft, shoplifting, handling stolen goods	113	3,940	2·9	48	1,026	4·7
Fraud, forgery	36	566	6·4	11	83	13·3
Other indictable offences	1	53	1·9	1	10	10·0
Total	306	7,076	4·3	66	1,194	5·5

MEDICAL DISPOSALS FOR INDICTABLE OFFENCES

The more careful screening procedure of Wessex magistrates was reflected in the proportions given medical disposals in the two areas. Medical treatment as part of the sentence of the court is usually imposed via a hospital order (Section 60, Mental Health Act, 1959) or via a probation order with a condition of treatment (Section 4, Criminal Justice Act, 1948). In Inner London, of the 2,404 persons medically remanded who had committed an indictable offence, 109 (4·5 per cent) received a hospital order and 66 (2·7 per cent) received a psychiatric probation order. In Wessex, on the other hand, the proportion of medical disposals was higher, for of the 372 medical remands, 25 (or 6·7 per cent) received a hospital order and 55 (or 15·1 per cent) received a psychiatric probation order.

The Wessex courts perhaps more readily distinguished offenders who could be dealt with by either a hospital order or a psychiatric probation order than did the Inner London courts, where more offenders were remanded but proportionately fewer medical disposals were made, but the relationship also applied to medical disposals in terms of total court turnover. Nine out of every thousand male offenders were given a medical disposal in Wessex, six per thousand in Inner London; the rates for females were respectively thirteen and seven per thousand.

Thus Inner London magistrates generally remanded a higher proportion of indictable offenders for a medical report than did their counterparts in Wessex. However, a lower proportion of the Inner London remands resulted in medical disposals and, although Inner London magistrates remanded many more persons, there were still a lower proportion of medical disposals than Wessex even in terms of the total court turnover. Some interpretations of these results are discussed towards the end of the next chapter.

The proportion of hospital orders was similar for both areas and for both sexes—Inner London being slightly higher, the largest number being imposed for males aged 30 or over (TABLE 7). Psychiatric probation orders were proportionally less used in Inner London—for each age group.

TABLE 7

PERCENTAGE OF MEDICAL DISPOSALS IN TERMS OF THE COURT TURNOVER BY SEX AND AGE (INDICTABLE OFFENCES ONLY)

Age	Males			Females		
	No. in Court Turnover	% Hospital Orders	% S 4 Probation Orders	No. in Court Turnover	% Hospital Orders	% S 4 Probation Orders
Inner London Magistrates' Courts						
17–20	5,785	0·21	0·14	1,281	0·08	0·55
21–29	8,170	0·32	0·15	1,766	0·40	0·51
30+	7,954	0·69	0·31	2,231	0·36	0·22
Total	21,909	0·42	0·20	5,278	0·30	0·40
Wessex Magistrates' Courts						
17–20	2,349	0·13	0·51	263	0·38	1·90
21–29	2,590	0·42	0·66	314	0·00	0·32
30+	2,137	0·42	0·56	617	0·16	0·97
Total	7,076	0·32	0·58	1,194	0·17	1·09*

* This total includes one woman whose age is unknown, but who received a psychiatric probation order.

The London figures suggested that more people appeared in London courts with *serious* disorders (that is, needing a hospital order) than did those with *mild* psychiatric disorders (that is, where a psychiatric probation order was thought to be beneficial). If so, this would imply a strange distribution of mental disorders, and the true situation is more likely that represented by the Wessex figures, where the number of minor disorders requiring psychiatric probation orders was about double that of more serious disorders requiring hospital orders.

There are, of course, various explanations for this.

(*a*) In London for milder cases of psychiatric disorder many more informal arrangements may have been made which did not need the formal imprint of the court even though they often received the court's blessing (for example the court would make a conditional discharge when an arrangement existed for admission under Section 25 or 26 of the Mental Health Act).

(*b*) Conversely, more London cases might have been dealt with by hospital order that elsewhere would have been dealt with by a psychiatric probation order, but this would imply a lower proportion of more seriously disturbed offenders in London than in Wessex.

(*c*) There might have been fewer mild disorders thought suitable for medical treatment in London. More probably the proportion of psychiatric probation orders in an area was related to the proportion remanded on bail for a medical report, and to the difficulty or otherwise of finding hospital places for seriously disturbed offenders. Regional variations in number and proportion of medical disposals were less a matter of the characteristics of offenders, and more a manifestation of the complex problem of communication between judiciary, administration, and doctors.

It has to be remembered that the psychiatrist is able to arrange medical treatment through an order of the court only for those remanded by the court for a medical report by him.[1] The proportion of medical disposals in each offence category, however, indicates whether there is any relationship between particular offences and persons officially labelled as mentally disordered. (The percentage of medical disposals as an outcome of *medical remands* is a separate issue and will be considered in the next chapter.)

It is evident from TABLE 8 that sexual offenders were the most likely to be labelled both 'criminal' and 'sick'. In London, a small proportion of the women committing offences of violence against the person were compulsorily detained by a hospital order, a psychiatric probation order not having been regarded as appropriate. On the other hand, 'offences against property with violence' when committed by females were likely to be regarded as a manifestation of psychiatric disturbance. In London, the tendency was to detain compulsorily by a hospital order, in Wessex to use a psychiatric probation order. Fraud and forgery was another category among female offenders where a medical disposal was higher than average. As these offences

---

[1] In fact this is not strictly true, for the psychiatrist may recommend a medical disposal in a psychiatric report completed for the defence. As we shall show in CHAPTER IX, this is a comparative rarity in the magistrates' court. Any medical disposals resulting solely from a defence submission have not been included in the analysis of the present chapter. Also, in a few cases the attention of the prison medical officer may be drawn to some persons being remanded in custody for other purposes, and he may decide to submit a voluntary report to the court in these circumstances.

TABLE 8
PERCENTAGE OF MEDICAL DISPOSALS IN TERMS OF THE COURT TURNOVER BY PRINCIPAL INDICTABLE OFFENCE

Principal Indictable Offence	Males			Females		
	No. in Court Turnover	% Hospital Orders	% S 4 Probation Orders	No. in Court Turnover	% Hospital Orders	% S 4 Probation Orders
Inner London Magistrates' Court						
Violence against the person	1,930	0·57	0·26	224	1·34	0·00
Sexual offences	589	1·02	1·02	—	—	—
Offences against property with violence	2,606	0·65	0·23	64	3·12	1·56
Unauthorized taking of motor vehicle	2,133	0·23	0·09	48	0·00	0·00
Theft, shoplifting, handling stolen goods	12,288	0·32	0·17	4,392	0·18	0·30
Fraud, forgery	2,199	0·64	0·18	515	0·58	1·36
Other indictable offences	164	0·61	0·61	35	0·00	0·00
Total	21,909	0·42	0·20	5,278	0·30	0·40
Wessex Magistrates' Courts						
Violence against the person	566	0·18	0·53	16	0·00	0·00
Sexual offences	178	3·37	3·37	1	0·00	0·00
Offences against property with violence	1,101	0·54	0·73	32	0·00	6·25
Unauthorized taking of motor vehicle	672	0·15	0·59	26	0·00	0·00
Theft, shoplifting, handling stolen goods	3,940	0·20	0·38	1,026	0·19	0·78
Fraud, forgery	566	0·18	0·88	83	0·00	3·61
Other indictable offences	53	0·00	0·00	10	0·00	0·00
Total	7,076	0·32	0·58	1,194	0·17	1·09

are often committed by young female drug addicts the comparatively high figure is unlikely to reflect a belief that medical treatment was useful for the offences *per se*.

COURT TURNOVER OF NON-INDICTABLE OFFENCES

A medical remand was unusual in respect of a non-indictable offence, and all that has been said about indictable offences applied even more to non-indictable offences in the two areas. Of the 167,352 non-indictable offences in the total Inner London court turnover in the year, 2,040 (1·2 per cent) offenders[1] were remanded either before or after trial for a medical report. In Wessex, there were only 180 medical remands (0·3 per cent) out of 55,212

[1] Persons who appear in court for both an indictable and non-indictable offence are counted twice (once in each section) in the Criminal Statistics of England and Wales. In order to use the court turnover figures, we had to follow a similar convention. Of the medical remands for non-indictable offences, one-quarter of these persons were also charged for indictable offences on the same occasion.

non-indictable cases. The use of police charge sheets in London and court registers in Wessex is likely to result in an under-estimate of medical remands in the Inner London area, so strengthening the belief that there was a real difference between the areas in terms of remanding for non-indictable offences.

TABLE 9

NUMBER AND PERCENTAGE OF MEDICAL REMANDS IN TERMS
OF SEX AND AGE (NON-INDICTABLE OFFENCES ONLY)

	Males			Females		
Age	No. of Medical Remands	No. in Court Turnover	% of Medical Remands	No. of Medical Remands	No. in Court Turnover	% of Medical Remands
Inner London Magistrates' Courts						
17–20	599	12,765	4·7	90	1,194	7·5
21	1,158	139,701	0·8	193	13,692	1·4
Total	1,757	152,466	1·2	283	14,886	1·9
Wessex Magistrates' Courts						
17–20	62	8,292	0·7	7	351	2·0
21	102	42,192	0·2	6	4,377	0·1
Total	167*	50,484	0·3	13	4,728	0·3

* Includes 3 cases for whom the ages were unknown.

Medical remands for non-indictable offences varied greatly with the offence. They were rare for drunkenness and more trivial non-indictable offences, probably because many of these offences cannot be followed directly by a sentence of imprisonment, and thus the powers of courts to remand or to give a medical disposal were restricted. Some non-indictable offences (sexual offences, malicious damage, begging, sleeping out, and drug offences) had a medical remand rate as high as, or higher than, indictable offences.

As TABLE 10 indicates, for each non-indictable offence category with the exception of drug offences, the proportion of male medical remands were lower in Wessex. The pattern is similar for females, but female medical remands for non-indictable offences in Wessex were so few (only 13) that comparisons are irrelevant. In other words, a difficult problem in London, namely, the number of women medically remanded for comparatively trivial non-indictable offences, was virtually unknown in Wessex.

MEDICAL DISPOSALS FOR NON-INDICTABLE OFFENCES

The pattern for non-indictable offences was similar to that for indictable offences. The apparently more careful screening process in Wessex seemed to be reflected in the proportions that received medical disposals in the two areas. In Inner London, of the 2,040 medical remands who had committed a non-indictable offence, 84 (4·1 per cent) received a hospital order and 39

TABLE 10

NUMBER AND PERCENTAGE OF MEDICAL REMANDS IN TERMS
OF PRINCIPAL NON-INDICTABLE OFFENCE

	Males			Females		
Principal Non-Indictable Offence	No. of Medical Remands	No. in Court Turnover	% of Medical Remands	No. of Medical Remands	No. in Court Turnover	% of Medical Remands
Inner London Magistrates' Courts						
Assault	145	3,076	4·7	10	811	1·2
Indecent exposure, offences by prostitutes, importuning by males	130	446	29·1	64	541	11·8
Drunkenness	148	28,865	0·5	48	3,133	1·5
Malicious damage	149	1,400	10·6	28	173	16·2
Disorderly behaviour	72	2,305	3·1	14	209	6·7
Prevention of Crimes Act, unlawful possession	155	1,822	8·5	19	84	22·6
Begging, sleeping out	55	249	22·1	10	31	32·3
Found on inclosed premises, frequenting	223	1,628	13·7	3	33	9·1
Drug offences	206	1,892	10·9	59	292	20·2
Motoring offences*	386	7,881	4·9	10	145	6·9
Other non-indictable offences	88	102,902	0·1	18	9,434	0·2
Total	1,757	152,466	1·2	283	14,886	1·9
Wessex Magistrates' Courts						
Assault	13	474	2·7	2	88	2·3
Indecent exposure, offences by prostitutes, importuning by males	15	143	10·5	1	34	2·9
Drunkenness	7	1,966	0·4	3	90	3·3
Malicious damage	21	547	3·8	2	16	12·5
Disorderly behaviour	4	211	1·9	1	9	11·1
Prevention of Crimes Act, unlawful possession	3	92	3·3	0	0	—
Begging, sleeping out	2	50	4·0	0	0	—
Found on inclosed premises, frequenting	3	70	4·3	0	1	0·0
Drug offences	47	262	17·9	2	17	11·8
Motoring offences	40	2,828	1·4	1	100	1·0
Other non-indictable offences	12	43,841	0·03	1	4,373	0·02
Total	167	50,484	0·3	13	4,728	0·3

* Motoring offences include Reckless or Dangerous Driving, Being in Charge of a Vehicle while Unfit, Vehicle Licence, and Insurance Offences.

(1·9 per cent) a psychiatric probation order. In Wessex, of the 180 medical remands, 9 (5·0 per cent) received a hospital order, and 14 (7·8 per cent) received a psychiatric probation order.

On this basis an area that remands a higher proportion of persons for a medical report should have a higher proportion of medical disposals in relation to court turnover. As TABLE 11 shows this was so for non-indictable offences unlike indictable offences (when Wessex did not have a higher proportion of medical disposals in relation to court turnover although fewer persons were remanded for a medical report).

TABLE 11

PERCENTAGE OF MEDICAL DISPOSALS IN TERMS OF THE COURT TURNOVER BY SEX AND AGE (NON-INDICTABLE OFFENCES ONLY)

Age	Males No. in Court Turnover	% Hospital Orders	% S4 Probation Orders	Females No. in Court Turnover	% Hospital Orders	% S4 Probation Orders
Inner London Magistrates' Courts						
17–20	12,765	0·047	0·031	1,194	0·167	0·167
21+	139,701	0·046	0·020	13,692	0·088	0·036
Total	152,466	0·046	0·021	14,886	0·094	0·040
Wessex Magistrates' Courts						
17–20	8,292	0·000	0·048	351	0·000	0·000
21+	42,192	0·021	0·024	4,377	0·000	0·000
Total	50,484	0·018	0·028	4,728	0·000	0·000

In Inner London, about seven in 10,000 male and 13 in 10,000 female non-indictable offenders received formal medical disposals in contrast to five in 10,000 males and no females in Wessex (it should be noted, of course, that in Wessex only 13 females were medically remanded for non-indictable offences, an indicator of reluctance there to consider medical treatment as a possible outcome for female non-indictable offenders).

Showing the proportion of hospital order as higher than that of psychiatric probation order as compared with Wessex may again mean that the mild disorders were fewer but was more likely due to a reluctance in London to consider this type of disposal. Moreover, for non-indictable offenders (where the sanctions available for many of the offences do not allow a compulsory hospital order under Section 60) many more informal arrangements were likely to be used. If the offence is trivial but recognized to be the behaviour of a psychiatrically disturbed individual, courts and doctors sometimes arrange a medical disposal that does not need the formal imprint of a court order (e.g. Section 25 or 26 of the Mental Health Act). This type of arrangement raises issues of civil liberties, for the offender appears to be deprived of his liberty (albeit in a hospital setting) for comparatively trivial behaviour. These issues are, of course, not peculiar to these individuals who are to some extent by-passing the court sanctions (but in reality receiving a custodial sanction rather than the non-custodial sentence that they might reasonably have expected!) but apply to all persons deprived of their liberty by medical intervention. These particular offenders are not detained for long in hospital and so on a practical level the issue of civil liberties is not major—in fact, most of the men and women for whom informal psychiatric arrangements were made, were probably deprived of their liberty for a longer time with a custodial remand while a decision was being made, than when the decision was put into action!

A wide range of behaviour is subsumed under the category of non-indictable offences. TABLE 12 indicates that for some non-indictable offence

TABLE 12

PERCENTAGE OF MEDICAL DISPOSALS IN TERMS OF THE COURT
TURNOVER BY PRINCIPAL NON-INDICTABLE OFFENCE

Principal Non-Indictable Offence	Males			Females		
	No. in Court Turnover	% Hospital Orders	% S4 Probation Orders	No. in Court Turnover	% Hospital Orders	% S4 Probation Orders
Inner London Magistrates' Courts						
Assault	3,076	0·45	0·03	811	0·00	0·00
Indecent exposure, offences by prostitutes, importuning by males	446	1·57	1·12	541	0·37	0·18
Drunkenness	28,865	0·00 (3)	0·02	3,133	0·00	0·03
Malicious damage	1,400	0·79	0·29	173	3·47	0·00
Disorderly behaviour	2,305	0·00	0·17	209	0·00	0·00
Prevention of Crimes Act, unlawful possession	1,822	0·99	0·16	84	2·38	1·19
Begging, sleeping out	249	1·20	0·40	31	0·00	3·23
Found on inclosed premises, frequenting	1,628	0·61	0·12	33	0·00	0·00
Drug offences	1,892	0·16	0·21	292	0·68	1·03
Motoring offences	7,881	0·02	0·00	145	0·00	0·00
Other non-indictable offences	102,902	0·00 (1)	0·00 (2)	9,434	0·02	0·00
Total	152,466	0·05	0·02	14,886	0·09	0·04
Wessex Magistrates' Courts						
Assault	474	0·21	0·00	88	0·00	0·00
Indecent exposure, offences by prostitutes, importuning by males	143	0·00	2·10	34	0·00	0·00
Drunkenness	1,966	0·00	0·00	90	0·00	0·00
Malicious damage	547	0·55	0·55	16	0·00	0·00
Disorderly behaviour	211	0·00	0·00	9	0·00	0·00
Prevention of Crimes Act, unlawful possession	92	0·00	0·00	0	—	—
Begging, sleeping out	50	2·00	0·00	0	—	—
Found on inclosed premises, frequenting	70	1·43	0·00	1	0·00	0·00
Drug offences	262	0·00	1·91	17	0·00	0·00
Motoring offences	2,828	0·03	0·00	100	0·00	0·00
Other non-indictable offences	43,841	0·00 (4)	0·01	4,373	0·00	0·00
Total	50,484	0·02	0·03	4,728	0·00	0·00

N.B. Figures in brackets refer to actual number of cases.

categories, particularly sexual offences, malicious damage and begging and sleeping out, the proportion of medical disposals was as high as, and sometimes higher than, that for some indictable offences. In fact, it demonstrates how the discussion of non-indictable offences has been influenced by 'other non-indictable offences' where a medical disposal was virtually unknown.

For certain types of behaviour in females the London courts readily imposed formal medical disposals whereas this procedure was not used for them in Wessex. For males, Wessex courts made a greater use of the psychiatric probation order: London courts in apparently similar cases tended to impose a compulsory hospital order. This certainly seemed true of sexual offenders: whereas in Wessex this was always a psychiatric probation order, in London a compulsory hospital order was imposed.

CONCLUSION

The medical remand was thus comparatively rare in the lower courts. The overall proportion of medical remands was between 2 and 3 per cent of the court turnover. However, whereas for indictable offences one in ten persons was remanded for a medical report, for non-indictable offences only one in a hundred persons was medically remanded. Non-indictable offence covered a large range of behaviour and, in fact, if trivial non-imprisonable offences (where perhaps one in a thousand persons are remanded for a medical report) are excluded, many non-indictable offences had a remand rate as high as, sometimes higher than, indictable offences.

These figures largely applied to London where a much higher proportion of persons was remanded for a medical report than in Wessex, where of those so remanded a higher proportion received a medical disposal. There are a number of explanations for this, but there is *prima facie* evidence that Wessex magistrates were more selective in their remands for a medical report. The higher proportion of medical disposals was accounted for by a greater willingness of Wessex psychiatrists to offer and of Wessex magistrates to impose psychiatric probation orders.

Though London magistrates remanded a higher proportion of persons for a medical report, Wessex nevertheless had a higher proportion of medical disposals even *in terms of the court turnover.* Ten out of a thousand indictable offenders dealt with by Wessex magistrates received a medical disposal, seven out of a thousand indictable offenders were so dealt with by Inner London magistrates. However, whereas Wessex magistrates medically remanded forty-five in each thousand indictable offenders, London magistrates medically remanded eighty-eight persons per thousand.

Comparisons can be misleading but a higher proportion of Wessex offenders was officially reported as suitable for psychiatric treatment. It is unlikely that Wessex contained more psychiatrically disordered offenders; it is much more likely that medical remand procedures rather than offenders differed in the two areas. Even if the offenders did differ, in the sense that more London cases 'needed' a medical remand, a much smaller proportion of them resulted in a medical disposal: Wessex magistrates made fewer and more suitable selections for a medical remand. This is important particularly in the light of the findings discussed in PART II that custodial remands, which form such a large proportion of London cases, have an unduly high proportion which the doctors considered 'unnecessary'.

CHAPTER IV

THE MEDICAL REMAND AND THE COURT PROCESS

IN the previous chapter we concluded that in Wessex the medical remand was used more satisfactorily than in London. We must remember, however, that the problem may lie in the numbers with which Inner London was attempting to deal. Accordingly, we shall consider the medical remand in more detail within the context of the court process. There are indeed indications that a different medical remand procedure had evolved in the two areas.

THE LOCUS OF THE OFFENCES

A police officer encounters very diverse behaviour in the course of his work, and will rapidly make a judgement about *prima facie* bizarre behaviour. Policemen will not necessarily agree in their recognition of bizarre behaviour or on their role in such situations. The police use of procedures to admit persons directly to hospital certainly varies with the area. In other words potential medical remands may be 'filtered off' before a charge is accepted by the station sergeant on duty, and such cases never reach the magistrates' court. As George (1972) confirms, incidents where the policeman takes immediate action under Section 136 of the Mental Health Act, 1959, tend to involve extremely bizarre behaviour. What is not known is what proportion of these incidents leads to a remand for a medical report, but for the Inner London sample we can consider the location of the offence for which 3,960 persons were subsequently remanded for a medical report.

The location of the principal offence varied for men and women: 41 per cent of the men and 33 per cent of the women in the sample committed their offence in open places. In contrast, 18 per cent of the men and 32 per cent of the women were subsequently remanded for a medical report for offences in 'schools, shops and hospitals'.

There was no comparable information on locus of the offence for Wessex, but most of the non-indictable offences were committed in 'open places' and the large number of these offences distinguished Inner London from Wessex. Both areas dealt with roughly six non-indictable offences for every indictable offence in the overall court turnover, but the ratio varied considerably in the proportions remanded. In Inner London the ratio for medical remands between indictable and non-indictable offences was almost one to one, in Wessex it was two to one. This discrepancy becomes important in the light of the large numbers involved in Inner London, and is a matter for administrative concern, especially as the homeless are more likely to be involved in trivial non-indictable offences so that a *custodial* remand becomes a necessity rather than an option. Considerably more persons in Inner London than in Wessex appeared before the courts for 'begging and/or sleeping out' and London magistrates referred a much higher proportion of these for a psychiatric examination (23 per cent in Inner London, 4 per cent in Wessex). In Inner London over sixty persons a year were remanded (inevitably in custody) for a medical report for begging and sleeping out, only two in Wessex. As the police in some parts of London used their powers extensively to take a person directly to hospital (so removing before the court hearing those who were most blatantly mentally ill), it was surprising that with the remainder London magistrates should have sought medical advice so much more frequently than their Wessex counterparts. Much of this discrepancy might be explained by the fact that Wessex magistrates had more information on which to base their decision *at the time of trial*, whereas the custodial remand after conviction was often the first occasion on which the London magistrate could obtain the information he needed.

POLICE BAIL OR CUSTODY

After the charge has been accepted by the duty officer at the police station, the station sergeant has to decide whether to keep the accused in police custody or release him on bail until his first court appearance.

TABLE 13 shows that in Inner London less than one-quarter of the cases

TABLE 13
POLICE BAIL BEFORE FIRST COURT APPEARANCE FOR INNER
LONDON SAMPLE

	Males		Females		Total	
	No.	*%*	*No.*	*%*	*No.*	*%*
Police bail	701	21·2	196	30·2	897	22·7
No bail [1]	1,824 [2]	55·1	319	49·1	2,143	54·1
Appeared same day [3]	785	23·7	135	20·8	920	23·2
Total	3,310	100·0	650	100·0	3,960	100·0

[1] The person was in custody in police cells at least overnight (i.e. since before midnight).

[2] The person was in custody in police cells since after midnight of the day of the first court appearance.

[3] This includes two men where there is incomplete information but it has been assumed in the analysis that they were in custody overnight.

subsequently remanded for a medical report obtained police bail, after being charged: the remainder were in police custody until their first court appearance. The table distinguishes between those taken into police custody before midnight and those taken in after midnight, for which the latter bail is more difficult.

A significantly higher proportion of females obtained police bail (Police Bail *v.* Others: $\chi2 = 25 \cdot 2$ I d.f. significant at $0 \cdot 1$ per cent), but the type of offence could well be crucial, for this is the sole criterion if the police wish to hold a person aged 17 years or over for longer than 24 hours. In the Inner London sample persons charged with indictable, rather than non-indictable offences had a slightly higher chance of receiving police bail after being charged; thus seriousness of offence was not the main criterion. Shoplifting, sexual offences, and taking and driving away of motor vehicles showed a higher rate of police bail. These groups tended to contain more offenders with addresses—this may be one of the criteria for granting of police bail. The 'low rate of bail' group contained the drunkenness offender, and the offender committing malicious damage or frequenting, i.e. offences associated with vagrancy and homelessness, but the drunkenness offender might have been too drunk to be bailed, and it might have been kinder to give a vagrant a bed and breakfast in a police cell than turn him back on to the street.

Time of charging is pertinent. The high proportion of shoplifters who were bailed might reflect the small number of them likely to be charged in the early hours of the morning. A defendant charged in the afternoon or early evening can more readily arrange sureties and the police can more easily make what checks they need before granting bail.

TABLE 14

RECOGNIZANCES AND SURETIES FOR THOSE OBTAINING
POLICE BAIL IN INNER LONDON SAMPLE

	Male		Female		Total	
	No.	%	No.	%	No.	%
Own Recognizances						
Less than £5	7	1·0	7	3·6	14	1·6
£5 but less than £10	12	1·7	6	3·1	18	2·0
£10 but less than £25	145	20·7	39	19·9	184	20·5
£25 but less than £50	208	29·7	65	33·2	273	30·4
£50 or more	134	19·1	31	15·8	165	18·4
Own Recognizance and one surety						
O/R and 1 surety less than £50 each	118	16·9	27	13·7	145	16·2
O/R and 1 surety £50 or more each	76	10·8	21	10·7	97	10·8
Own Recognizances and two or more sureties (any amount)	1	0·1	—	—	1	0·1
Total	701	100·0	196	100·0	897	100·0

Other factors are thus more relevant than 'seriousness' of offence: type of offender, for instance. Police bail was never given for begging and sleeping out, and King (1971) has emphasized the problems of drug offenders in obtaining bail, suggesting that police and courts regard drug offenders as 'serious cases'. The police almost certainly take many more factors into account than 'seriousness' of the offence.

For those released on bail by the police before their court appearance a considerable range of recognizances and sureties was requested, as TABLE 14 indicates. There was evidence of differential granting of bail between male and female suspects but little difference about the terms once the decision to grant police bail had been reached. For these offences (all tried subsequently at the magistrates' court level) a request for two sureties was virtually never insisted upon but in approximately one-quarter of the cases for both males and females, one surety was requested. When bail was granted, a higher proportion of persons charged with indictable offences required a surety than was the case for non-indictable offences; 'seriousness' of the offence was thus more likely to influence the amount of recognizances and/or sureties required than to influence the granting of bail.

THE COURT PHASE

FIRST COURT APPEARANCE

As a solicitor, King (1971) strongly emphasizes the legal implications of how police and defendant use the time between arrest and first court appearance. Martin and Webster (1971) as sociologists, tend to emphasize the importance of police bail in relation to the subsequent proceedings. Those bailed have had a better opportunity to discuss recent events with friends and relations, and prepare for the court appearance, and are more likely to be regarded as ordinary members of the public. The defendant is in a more favourable position, 'waiting in the corridor outside court, smoking a cigarette, talking to his witnesses, and studying the court-list on the wall giving the names and addresses of persons appearing that day, one of a miscellaneous crowd of defendants, witnesses, police officers, a probation officer, and others'. By contrast, those who have spent a night in custody are usually tired and drawn, and feel and look more like a member of the prison population than someone who had been at liberty fewer than twenty-four hours or so before. Other commentators have emphasized the importance of the initial police action in terms of whether the defendants are subsequently remanded in custody or on bail after the first court appearance. The influence of police bail or custody on the court's decision to adjourn the case for a medical examination and report may have been under-estimated. Bizarre or violent behaviour can be much more cogently explained by a clean-shaven defendant who has had a night's rest and is wearing a clean shirt, than by a tired unshaven and unkempt defendant who has spent at least a night in police custody.

The first appearance in court was decisive for the majority in the Inner London sample. Decisions about sexual offences and shoplifting were reached more quickly than for most other indictable offences. Of the offenders eventually remanded for a medical report, two-thirds were both convicted and medically remanded on their first court appearance. Drunkenness, malicious damage, disorderly behaviour, begging and sleeping out tended to be non-indictable offences quickly dealt with by London magistrates and the proportions in these categories for conviction and remand for medical

TABLE 15

OUTCOME OF FIRST APPEARANCE FOR INNER LONDON SAMPLE

	Male		Female		Total	
	No.	%	No.	%	No.	%
First Court Appearance						
Convicted and remanded for a medical report	2,169	65·5	455	70·0	2,624	66·3
Convicted but remanded subsequently for a medical report	104	3·2	19	2·9	123	3·1
Remanded for a pre-trial medical report	205	6·2	48	7·4	253	6·4
Neither convicted nor remanded for a medical report	832	25·1	128	19·7	960	24·2
Total	3,310	100·0	650	100·0	3,960	100·0

reports on first court appearance were similar. Drug offences were an exception to this: only 41 out of 233 (18 per cent) were both convicted and remanded for a medical report on this first court appearance. Drug offences, however, entail allowing time during the proceedings for the analysis of substances.

TOTAL TIME FROM FIRST COURT APPEARANCE TO DATE OF SENTENCE

Our study by definition excludes offenders dealt with entirely at the first court appearance. APPENDIX 3 gives for the Inner London sample the total time involved from first court appearance to date of sentence.

For both sexes 70 per cent of the cases involving a medical remand were completed within one month of the first court appearance, but the length of time taken to complete the court proceedings varies with type of offence. For example, only 30 per cent of drug offence cases were concluded within a month.

For the defendant, whether the period between the first court appearance in court and the date of sentence is spent on bail or in custody is important. Long periods awaiting trial or sentence are undesirable and long periods in custody are likely to be more damaging than long periods on bail awaiting an outcome.

Some cases fluctuated between bail and custody from appearance to appearance, but 72 per cent in Inner London spent no time on bail during the court process. The longer the court process the greater the tendency for the proportion of persons held in custody throughout to fall. With those court processes that took fewer than eight days, all 173 defendants remanded just for this period were remanded in custody, but with court processes that last between 51 and 71 days, 81 of the 261 persons involved (31 per cent) were remanded in custody throughout the period. A sizeable proportion of the sample had to remain in custody for a month or more (see APPENDIX 4).

The subsequent sentence of persons remanded in custody was relevant, particularly if it was non-custodial. A custodial remand may sometimes be necessary even if the offence is not 'serious' enough to warrant a custodial sentence, but these occasions should be the exception. In fact, if the persons in the sample who were sentenced at a higher court (i.e. those that the magistrate had not sufficient powers to deal with) are disregarded, 69 per cent of all those remanded in custody throughout received a non-custodial sentence, 10 per cent received a medical disposal (i.e. psychiatric probation order or a hospital order), and 21 per cent were subsequently sent either to prison or to a 'young offender' institution.

THE MEDICAL REMAND

The request for medical evidence is, of course, only one reason why a case is not dealt with immediately. We found the period of the medical remand to coincide exactly with the total time between first court appearance and date of sentence for 1952 (59 per cent) of the males and 408 (63 per cent) of the females. Even for these the remand might not have been solely for a medical report, for the court might at the same time have requested other types of report. Of the 2,360, 1,413 men and 293 women were remanded for probation reports at the same time and for the same length of time as the medical remand. Conversely, no other reports were requested by the magistrates in one-quarter of the cases; thus for a sizeable minority at least, the medical remand was the sole reason for adjournment during the court process.

Two important distinctions must be made about the medical remand— whether it is pre- or post-trial and whether it is in custody or on bail. The implications of bail and custodial medical remand differ for the defendant and for the court. For the defendant a custodial remand is as much a deprivation of liberty as is imprisonment. He can be excused for believing that the decision to remand him in custody for two or three weeks is arbitrary. For the court, on the other hand, a custodial remand has benefits. It is not difficult to arrange, for the prison medical officers are geared to providing a service for the courts; in other words, the medical report will be received in court on the appointed day and the doctor is unlikely to report to the court that the defendant failed to arrive for an appointment. The undoubted administrative convenience of the custodial remand is often justified by more doubtful arguments. In some courts there is the belief that it is more appropriate to remand offenders in custody for a medical report, on the grounds that a qualitatively better report will be received. Prison medical officers have experience in dealing with offenders and custody offers an opportunity for continual observation to increase the value of the report, it is argued. In fact, prison medical officers have to persuade *hospital consultants* to accept an offender for treatment and prison is inappropriate for observation under free conditions. Courts that remand a high proportion of offenders on bail for a medical report consider the advantages of their procedure to outweigh the administrative convenience of a custodial remand.

PRE- AND POST-TRIAL REMANDS

In Inner London 289 offenders were remanded for a pre-trial medical report; 31 of these were remanded again after conviction for a second report. The majority (93 per cent) of offenders were only remanded for a post-trial medical report. The sexes differed little (TABLE 16) in this, but the pre-trial medical remand was rare in Wessex.[1] Fewer than one medical remand in a hundred was pre-trial in Wessex, whereas in Inner London, the proportion was seven out of every hundred.

TABLE 16

COMPARISON OF INNER LONDON AND WESSEX AREAS IN TERMS OF THE FIRST TYPE OF MEDICAL REMAND

Type of Medical Remand*	Males		Females	
	Inner London %	Wessex %	Inner London %	Wessex %
Pre-trial	6·9	0·7	9·1	1·3
Post-trial	93·1	99·3	90·1	98·7
Total	100·0	100·0	100·0	100·0
Total No. of persons	3,310	413	650	77

* In this table the first type of medical remand is shown, so if a person is remanded for a medical report both pre-trial and post-trial, he is shown as 'pre-trial' remand in this particular analysis.

This is largely explained by the predominance of the non-indictable offence in Inner London: 49 per cent of the male and 31 per cent of the female pre-trial remands in Inner London were for non-indictable offences. Thus the non-indictable offences (where the weighting given to culpability may be less than for indictable offences) had a higher rate of pre-trial remanding. However, whether indictable or non-indictable, offences classified as violent, assaultive, or disorderly dominated the pre-trial picture. Bizarre or manifestly disturbed behaviour might have been easily most identifiable in these cases.

London magistrates used the pre-trial medical remand with more frequency

[1] In fact, for the year 1969, there is evidence of only 4 pre-trial medical reports being requested throughout Wessex out of a total of 490 medical requests.

than their Wessex counterparts, but the eighteen Inner London courts showed a considerable range of pre-trial remanding practices, not entirely accounted for by the type of offence that came before the individual courts. One London court remanded before trial a quarter of all persons remanded for a medical report; the next highest rate was 10 per cent; in some London courts the rate fell below 1 per cent.

The pre-trial group formed an important extension of the groups mentioned in CHAPTER I, individuals dealt with either informally or under Section 136 of the Mental Health Act 1959. It is difficult to ascertain whether the variation between London courts in use of pre-trial remand was due to a police reluctance to use their powers or to the magistrates readiness to use theirs. It is clear, however, that considerable numbers of offender-patients were identified at the pre-trial stage. In 21 per cent of the pre-trial remands, either the cases were adjourned or the charges were withdrawn or dismissed (with the strong possibility that a Section 25 Mental Health Act 1959 order would be made) as compared with less than 1 per cent for the post-trial medical remands. Likewise, hospital orders (Section 60) were made for 16 per cent of the pre-trial group but for only 5 per cent of the post-trial group. Pre-trial remands in London were a distinct group. In Wessex these types of offender did not exist or were dealt with differently.

REMANDS IN CUSTODY OR ON BAIL

A remand in custody can cause hardship and upset to a defendant and several reports—more especially Zander (1967) and Davies (1969)—suggest that the custodial remand may often by unwarranted or due to the magistrates' failure to obtain information that would have made a remand on bail more appropriate. Few reports mention the remand for medical reports— exceptions include Sparks (1966) and Dell and Gibbens (1971)—and those that do generally fail to consider geographical differences. The Cambridge Study on *Sexual Offences* (Radzinowicz, 1957) in describing the situation in the early 1950s noted that 'in areas outside the metropolis and larger cities, it was frequently difficult to obtain a medical report unless the offender was remanded in custody'. The present evidence suggests that the position is almost totally reversed. In Wessex the proportion of remands on bail for a medical report was higher than in London (TABLE 17). This also applied to males and females taken separately, and moreover the proportion in Wessex for males was higher than those for females in Inner London.

The use of pre-trial remands in Inner London (pre-trial remands were almost invariably in custody) might have exaggerated the difference. If all the pre-trial remands are disregarded highly significant differences between the areas in terms of the location of post-trial remands nevertheless remain.

In London 476 persons, *only just over half the numbers given bail by the police after being charged*, had at least one medical remand on bail, which suggests that courts were more cautious about granting bail than were the police. Unless the police had reversed their attitude by opposing bail in court in cases where they had previously released on bail the diminishing in the numbers remanded on bail for a medical report must have been due to the court's acting on its own initiative rather than supporting the police opposition. Thus courts might have had different criteria for the custody/bail decision when a medical remand was involved than in other cases.

TABLE 17

COMPARISON OF INNER LONDON AND WESSEX AREAS IN TERMS OF FIRST TYPE OF MEDICAL REMAND—WHETHER IN CUSTODY OR BAIL

First type of medical remand	Males		Females	
	Inner London %	Wessex %	Inner London %	Wessex %
First medical remand on bail	9·5	35·4	22·8	44·2
First medical remand in custody	90·5	64·6	77·2	55·8
Total	100·0	100·0	100·0	100·0
Total No. of persons	3,310	413	650	77

Inner London versus Wessex

Males   Bail v. Custody $\chi^2 = 208\cdot2$ 1 d.f.   Significant at 0·1 per cent level
Females   Bail v. Custody $\chi^2 = 13\cdot9$ 1 d.f.   Significant at 0·1 per cent level

In Wessex not only were there more medical remands on bail but the bail conditions were less stringent: 29 per cent of the cases were remanded on bail for recognizances of less than £10, whereas in Inner London only 4 per cent were so remanded. Of those remanded on bail for a medical report sureties were required for 24 per cent in Inner London, but for only 9 per cent in Wessex. King (1971) discusses sureties in some detail: the Inner London 24 per cent is considerably lower than his overall London figure of 40 per cent.

DISCUSSION

This section has demonstrated large differences between the Inner London and Wessex samples in the extent and type of the medical remand. In Wessex the pre-trial remand was rare (four cases throughout the whole year); in Inner London it was used in at least 289 cases (7 per cent of the total). The use of the medical remand on bail was much more widespread in Wessex; only 12 per cent of those in the Inner London sample were remanded on bail for a medical report whereas 37 per cent were so remanded in Wessex.

One particular type of offender appearing before the Inner London courts presented a problem virtually unknown in Wessex. This was the 'social nuisance'. The fact that London magistrates, justifiably or not, remanded this type of person into custody begins to account for some of the differences in the proportions bailed in the two areas. Nevertheless, Wessex made a higher proportion of remands on bail *whatever the type of offence*. Whereas Inner London remanded on bail for a medical report only a tenth of the malicious damage cases, Wessex remanded on bail twice that proportion. This pattern was repeated for each offence category for both males and females.

There are two possible implications. Inner London offenders might have been consistently less suitable for remanding on bail, i.e. drunks in London were less suitable than drunks in Wessex; London thieves less bailable than Wessex thieves; London sexual offenders a greater risk than Wessex sexual offenders and so on, but the pattern was too consistent for such an overall explanation, and although there was police evidence that many of those remanded in custody for a medical report were 'bailable' the request for a report necessitated a *custodial* remand. 3,497 persons (88 per cent) of the Inner London sample were remanded in custody for a medical report and of these, 2,847 were held in custody throughout the court process: 424 (15 per cent) of those held in custody throughout the court process had received police bail, not much below the overall percentage of 22·7 per cent given police bail in the Inner London sample. However, this still left 650 who had a medical remand in custody but a period on bail at some time during the same court process. 489 cases (75 per cent) of these were given a period on bail by the court before the magistrates decided to remand in custody for a medical report.

To summarize, if police bail and court bail received before the medical request was included, *one-quarter of those remanded in custody for a medical report had had either police or court bail before the medical remand* (the proportions were identical for males and females). Remand in custody after some time spent on bail might have been because of a breach of the recognizances imposed by police or court, but this applied to only a small minority. More probably, the remand in custody for a medical report was, in London, unconnected with the defendant's likely attendance in court. The use of bail varied fairly widely between London courts: one remanded over 80 per cent into custody throughout the court process, another remanded 54 per cent on bail at least at some stage of the court proceedings. The busiest London courts had the highest rates of custodial remanding. Where speed is important the custodial remand is dangerously easy to administer.

It is possible, of course, that the offenders remanded on bail differed in the two areas, but the explanation is much more likely to lie in a difference in remanding practices, because even when allowance is made for the fact that Inner London had a much higher proportion of problematical 'social nuisance' offenders, Wessex nevertheless had more remands on bail.

Remanding in custody, though unpleasant and expensive, is nevertheless sometimes necessary. What is questionable was the necessity in London for the remand in custody for a medical report to be the rule rather than the exception. Were London magistrates justified in pursuing so diligently their preference for the custodial remand?

Two issues are involved. In the first place, were the offenders suitable for remanding on bail? Many could have been remanded on bail with only a minimal risk that they would fail to appear at the adjourned hearing, but the magistrates might have considered bail after conviction to be a greater risk than before conviction. There was no evidence for this, and *a priori* it was unlikely because most defendants plead guilty and know the limitations of the sentencing powers of the courts for their offence. Most are likely to know that the remand period will be the longest time that they will spend in prison.

London magistrates might agree that a proportion of the persons they remanded in custody for a medical report could have been remanded on bail. Perhaps the issue was more complicated than a comparatively straightforward custody/bail decision, for it might reflect the special nature of this type of remand. Given that some 'good risks' in London are at present remanded in custody for a medical report, some magistrates may argue that they cannot remand on bail because facilities for obtaining a medical report are inadequate for the potential need. We have no doubt that the bail facilities and greater involvement of hospital consultants in forensic work in Wessex were a key factor which supports the view that Wessex was dealing with the medical remand in a more satisfactory manner than was London. However, since the time of the present study, out-patient facilities have been provided at certain London prisons; but seem to be consistently under-used. Insufficient bail facilities are not the only reason why 'good risks' are remanded in custody for a medical report. Certain magistrates may believe prisons or remand centres to be the most appropriate place for observing the defendant and ensuring that the court receives the most appropriate medical recommendations. Some magistrates also believe that the prison medical staff have a special competence in the field of offender behaviour and in this belief they remand even very 'good risks' in custody for a medical report. Clearly, if such beliefs prevail, to provide bail facilities for a medical report will only marginally modify the numbers remanded in custody for this purpose.

Some commentators have suggested that some magistrates may use the period on remand for 'punitive' purposes. This suggestion has developed some force in recent years, for if certain sentencing possibilities are blocked magistrates may try to find other ways of producing the same outcome. Magistrates often say that the fact that an offender has spent several weeks in custody on remand enables them to take a lenient view when he returns to court. Given that some magistrates manipulate the system in some way, there are still two possibilities; they may remand in custody for a medical report persons that they would otherwise remand on bail or they may remand in custody for a medical report (with the possibility of three weeks in custody) persons who would otherwise not be remanded for a medical report at all. In Wessex, the latter alternative was rarely, if ever, used if a medical report was unnecessary. However, it could be argued that a medical report could be interesting and useful for practically every offender appearing before the court. Though this is not necessarily valid it indicates how carefully the purpose of the medical remand should be examined.

The development of a 'treatment ethic' by the courts could produce the corollary that a medical remand would be useful for every offender. This tendency could be disastrous not only for the offender but for the working of the courts. A more appropriate question would be why a medical remand at all? When this has been resolved the next issue would be that of bail or custody. The criteria for bail suitability for the medical remand are similar to those for any other type of remand.[1]

THE OUTCOME OF THE MEDICAL REMAND: THE SENTENCE OF THE COURT

The final phase is the determination of the appropriate sentence. In arriving at their decisions for the persons in our sample, the bench obviously were able to consider medical reports provided after remand by the court for this purpose. In CHAPTER III we indicated that only for a small proportion

---

[1] Since this report was prepared a valuable paper has been published (Faulk & Trafford, *The Efficacy of Medical Remands*, 1975) which provides a commentary on the use of custody. The first author holds one of the new 'joint-appointments' between the prison service and the National Health Service. It dealt with all the 29 cases remanded in custody for psychiatric reports from the Southampton Magistrates' Court (21 cases) and from Southampton Crown Court (8 cases) during a six month period, excluding young offenders (admitted to the remand centre)—not a large number. As they say, 'Inquiry indicated that courts in the Southampton region do not remand cases in custody simply to facilitate reporting ... in general, psychiatrists in the town were able to provide all the reports requested for men on bail, within a reasonable period of time for the courts'. Only one of the 29 cases 'slipped through due to administrative error'. Of the 29, 60 per cent had had previous psychiatric care and two-thirds had been in a penal institution in the past, usually in prison. The value of the wide experience of the joint-appointment consultants inside and outside prison is shown by the fact that the recommendations were followed in 24 cases and these consisted of probation, with or without psychiatric treatment, hostel placement, or supervision, in half the cases; voluntary psychiatric treatment in three, Section 60 hospital order in two, psychiatric treatment in prison in two cases. Above all 'the clinicians involved were able to take responsibility for the treatment of the cases they saw from Southampton either in prison or in the out-patient department, and this factor, above every other, may have been responsible for the high percentage of the medical disposals'. From our present point of view, the comments of the authors on the 'function of prison during remand period' was of great interest, bearing in mind that about a quarter were Crown Court cases. 'It was acting as a simple bail hostel for those who found themselves with no fixed address—10 cases (or a third); as a secure bail hostel for those who had already broken bail—six cases; as an acute alcoholic admission unit for those who required medical supervision while drying out from severe alcohol abuse—seven cases; and as an acute psychiatric ward for those with severe mental disturbance—six cases.' 'The remand situation fulfils a number of different functions, e.g bail hostel, alcoholic unit, or acute psychiatric ward. It has a very important job as a back-stop to the community.' No one will doubt the reality of this view, and the authors make the telling point that if these functions were immediately transferred to the community (as one hopes they ultimately will) 'the new units, like the hospitals, will become selective and therefore not able completely to meet the task'. They imply that it is proving possible to start the development of hostels only because they do not have to deal with the most awkward potential inmates. Nevertheless, their stated results show that the developing hostels and detoxification units could and no doubt should ultimately obviate remanding in custody no less than 58 per cent of the carefully selected cases in the Wessex area.

of persons was this evidence available to the courts before sentencing and that medical disposals were only a small proportion of court turnover.

The differences between the proportions that received a medical disposal in the two areas were large for as TABLE 18 shows, 8 per cent of the men were given a hospital order or a psychiatric probation order in Inner London, 22 per cent in Wessex; for females the relationship was similar.

TABLE 18

COMPARISON OF INNER LONDON AND WESSEX IN TERMS OF MEDICAL SENTENCE

	Males		Females	
Sentence	Inner London %	Wessex %	Inner London %	Wessex %
Probation Order (S4 CJ 1948)	2·6	13·6	4·5	18·2
Hospital Order (S60 MHA 1969)	5·2	8·3	5·2	2·6
Total of medical sentences	7·8	21·9	9·7	20·8
All other sentences	92·2	78·1	90·3	79·2
Total	100·0	100·0	100·0	100·0
Total number of persons	3,310	413	650	77

Medical sentences: Inner London v. Wessex.

Males

Medical sentences v. all other sentences: $\chi^2 = 88\cdot0$ 1 d.f. sig. at 0·1 per cent level
Hospital orders v. all other sentences: $\chi^2 = 6\cdot3$ 1 d.f. sig. at 0·5 per cent level
Probation orders (S4) v. all other sentences: $\chi^2 = 117\cdot3$ 1 d.f. sig. at 0·1 per cent level

Females

Medical sentences v. all other sentences: $\chi^2 = 8\cdot6$ 1 d.f. sig. at 1·0 per cent level
Hospital orders v. all other sentences: $\chi^2 = 1\cdot2$ 1 d.f. N.S.
Probation orders (S4) v. all other sentences: $\chi^2 = 19\cdot5$ 1 d.f. sig. at 0·1 per cent level

The sentences imposed differed in the two areas, for custodial sentences the proportions were: males, 27 per cent in Inner London; 22 per cent in Wessex; females, 10 per cent in Inner London, 8 per cent in Wessex. In view of the number remanded in custody for a medical report, the small proportion of *custodial sentences* was interesting. Over two-thirds of the present sample received a non-custodial sentence, which suggests that the medical remand was not used solely for the more serious offences. In other words, the main purpose was to discover those in need of medical treatment.[1] The comparatively trivial nature of many of the offences committed by the Inner London sample is reflected in the fact that 15 per cent of the males and 20 per cent of the females were either bound over or discharged absolutely or conditionally (Wessex 6 per cent and 12 per cent). 18 per cent of the Inner London males and 25 per cent of the Wessex males received a

[1] It is, of course, true that a hospital order is normally only possible for persons committing imprisonable offences, but this makes only a marginal difference to the above argument.

probation order. In both areas the proportion for females was just over one-third. About 13 per cent of both sexes were fined in both areas. The suspended sentence was slightly more used in Inner London than in Wessex and more for males than for females (see APPENDIX 5).

Most of the difference between the areas in medical disposal was in the greater use in Wessex of psychiatric probation orders. The figures for hospital orders, however, were similar for both areas and for both sexes and any small differences were probably due to chance.

The much higher rate of medical disposal in Wessex might have several explanations. Wessex magistrates might have been better at selection. This was unlikely in that because of the numbers dealt with London stipendiary magistrates should have been more experienced in spotting offenders in need of medical treatment than their Wessex colleagues. However, it must be remembered that Wessex magistrates had more information about the defendant on which to decide. Many courts were provided with pre-trial social inquiries by the probation service, and because of the local social structure an offender was less likely to come before a Wessex court totally unknown. Less pressure on the work of the court might have given more time to reach an appropriate decision. There is no doubt that the London magistrates had to make far-reaching decisions on scanty information.

Another possible explanation may lie in differences in the populations remanded in the two areas. Inner London had an intractable 'stage army' of offenders probably unmatched elsewhere in England. They were only a marginal problem for the Wessex courts. The London courts desperately need a solution to the problem of the many men and women who are a social problem but in the psychiatric view less amenable to medical treatment than the court would hope. It is impossible to take into account statistically all the reasons for a remand for a medical report. There is certainly no such thing as a 'correct' proportion of medical disposals for each group of offenders medically remanded.

Again, Wessex psychiatrists might have been more willing to help in the medical treatment of offenders appearing before the courts—or those medically remanded by the courts. There is probably some truth in this, for as will be shown in PART II a high proportion of Wessex hospital consultants were involved in the local forensic work as indicated by the higher proportion of psychiatric probation orders in Wessex. The proportions for whom a hospital order was recommended were similar in both areas but London had fewer mild cases (i.e. those for whom a psychiatric probation order was imposed) than serious cases. London consultants and/or medical officers in London prisons could, of course, have had a different conception of the use of the psychiatric probation orders from that of their Wessex colleagues; or there might have been fewer appropriate cases for the psychiatric probation order in London. Moreover the social derelicts who appeared so frequently on the London scene were fewer in Wessex. Equally the Wessex psychiatrists might also have benefited from the greater information presented to the Wessex courts.

As a final point it should be noted that a medical remand on bail in Wessex for either males or females made the likelihood of a subsequent medical disposal quite high, for this occurred with one in four of the males, and over one in five of the females, remanded on bail. Greater involvement by hospital consultants in the medical remand seemed to produce a greater willingness to offer medical treatment. The greater the number of cases seen by psychiatrists the higher was the *proportion* of medical disposals. This suggests that a greater involvement of the hospital consultant in the remand situation may increase the options open to the court when the offender is sentenced.

PART II:
THE PROSPECTIVE STUDY
WESSEX 1970-1

CHAPTER V

INTRODUCTION

As explained in CHAPTER II, the broad statistical study of remands in Inner London and Wessex in 1969 was followed by a more detailed study of Wessex in 1970-1 made possible by the smaller numbers, the homogeneity of the services and the co-operation of the doctors.

The plan involved (1) a careful check by all the forty or so consultant psychiatrists and prison medical officers on all the offenders they reported upon during the survey period and the completion of a detailed questionnaire about them. (2) The probation officers' social reports in each case and (3) probation reports upon a male 'control' group, consisting of the next male case not medically remanded on whom the probation officer concerned prepared a report. (4) The previous check on the court records was maintained to make sure no cases were lost, and to find out the outcome of the remand.

This method was maintained for eight months (1 September 1970-30 April 1971) and yielded 287 men and 56 women remanded in custody or on bail for a medical report. Questionnaires were completed in 89 per cent of men and 77 per cent of women[1] but the probation reports were, for various reasons, only obtained in 45 per cent of the cases and 40 per cent of the controls.

CHANGES BETWEEN 1969 AND 1970-1

In what follows we shall treat the eight month sample as the total sample, but in one respect it was interesting to work out what the total sample would have been in a full year. This showed a considerable increase in medical remands between 1969 and the winter of 1970-1; 4 per cent among men and 9 per cent for women, distinctly above the national rate of increase (though the national figures refer only to remands in custody).

We had expected the situation to remain relatively stable from 1969 to 1970, and this degree of change raised the question of a possible change in the sample for the detailed prospective study and of the causes of this. Comparison of the Wessex results for 1969 suggested that the increase had

---

[1] Some female cases were overlooked because it was not appreciated that they had been sent to Pucklechurch Remand Centre.

been a general one and that the population concerned had been very similar. The proportion of males to females was the same, there were only slight changes in the age distribution, very slightly more males had been in breach of previous court orders than in 1969, the proportion offending singly or in groups had not changed, and there was no significant difference in the types of offence committed.

The most remarkable change, however, was the significant increase in the proportion remanded on bail rather than in custody, which for both sexes together rose from 37 per cent to 45 per cent ($\chi^2 = 6\cdot67$ significant at 1 per cent level). For males the increase from 35 per cent to 41 per cent although noticeable, was not statistically significant, but for females the increase was from 44 per cent to 68 per cent, highly significant. Remand of women on bail had now become the rule rather than the exception.

One can only speculate about the reasons for this rapid change. It might be attributed to the 'Hawthorne effect' by which the knowledge that research is going on has been observed to change current practice and attitudes, or response to treatment. But although all the doctors knew of the study and that bail or custody was a matter of interest, the decision did not lie with them and it is unlikely that the many scores of magistrates had heard of the study, or been influenced by it if they had. The probable explanation is that the Criminal Justice Act of 1967 was starting to have effect. As explained in the introduction, this Act (Section 18) restricts the use of custody for remand under Section 14 with certain exceptions (that the offender has been in prison before, has estreated bail, has no fixed address, has committed a crime of violence etc.). Section 18 (6) says that this restriction does *not* apply to medical remands 'if it appears to the court that it would be impracticable to obtain such a report without remanding the defendant in custody'. The Wessex magistrates may have realized that remand on bail was not impracticable in a majority of cases.

THE INVOLVEMENT OF PSYCHIATRISTS IN FORENSIC WORK

A consultant psychiatrist may be involved in forensic work in many different ways. He may report upon an offender as an outpatient on bail; it may be a new case or one that he has formerly treated or still treats. He may be asked by the solicitor for the defence or by a probation officer to see an accused person, either while on remand or after a standard probation order has been made. If an offender is in custody he may be asked by the prison medical officer to visit the prison to see if he will agree to treat the offender on probation (in-patient or out-patient) or admit him under a hospital order (Section 60) or a 28-day order (Section 25) and to complete the necessary certificates; or to see an offender for the defence. As a visiting psychotherapist to the prison he may be asked for a formal or informal second opinion.

For the moment our concern is to describe the involvement of consultant psychiatrists and prison medical officers in the initial remand process, and to discuss such matters as the number of consultants involved in the region, and for bail cases how quickly the medical report could be prepared, where the offender was interviewed, how often, and so on. It must be emphasized that we are only dealing with magistrates' court cases and not high court cases.

There were in the sample 343 offenders (287 males and 56 females) and the main division was between the 118 (41 per cent) males and 38 (68 per cent) females seen by consultants on bail and the remainder seen in the first instance by the prison medical officer in custody. In five bail cases a medical report on bail was requested but not submitted, because of death, illness or absence of the patient or doctor, and the court decided that it had enough information to proceed without one.

THE WORK OF HOSPITAL CONSULTANTS

Of the remaining 338 persons, 151 were seen in the first instance on bail. They were seen by 39 consultants, of which seven were attached to hospitals outside the Wessex Regional Hospital Board area.

Virtually all the consultants in the region had some dealings with forensic cases. Only nine did not give a first report upon a bail case from a magistrates' court during the eight months; but nearly all of these were involved in other ways. Two were visiting psychotherapists to the prisons and were frequently consulted informally. Others saw cases for the defence, were called to the prison in consultation on specialized aspects—subnormality, alcoholism or drug addiction; one was also a local magistrate, who can hardly be described as not involved in forensic work! There was no evidence of involvement in respect of one or possibly two consultants, one of whom expressed a dislike for court work.

The majority of consultants were not involved to a great extent. Table 19 shows that the great majority did not report on a bail case more often than once in two months and only four averaged one or more a month.

TABLE 19 reveals a state of affairs of fundamental importance to forensic psychiatry. Some psychiatrists because of their interest in the work and

TABLE 19
NUMBER OF MEDICAL REPORTS ON BAIL SUBMITTED BY
PSYCHIATRISTS IN EIGHT MONTHS

No. of Reports	No. of Psychiatrists	Total No. of Reports
1–4	22	46
5–8	6	40
9 or more	4	52
	32	138*

* These figures disregard those seen by psychiatrists outside the region and those where the psychiatrist's name was not given.

extensive experience which probably commends them to lawyers, take a major share in forensic work. One senior consultant played a special role in this development, being actively engaged in magistrates' and high court cases and in defence work.

Personal interest, however, is perhaps not the only factor. Some consultants are in charge of many more beds for men than for women, some have male wards with a nursing staff experienced in dealing with, for example, chronic psychotic patients who show considerable behaviour disorders. They are more willing and able to receive mentally abnormal offenders and have suitable physical facilities for them. The prison medical officers tend to call in these consultants. Their opinion will be sought about other cases and they will be recommended to solicitors. Those in charge of female beds will have other social problems brought to their notice—marriage guidance, abortion, family planning, or perhaps the middle-aged woman shoplifter.

A second factor is that medical secretaries soon learn of the interests and preferences of consultants, and, unless in the hospital new appointments are allocated to consultants in strict rotation, patients tend to be allocated to consultants known to be interested in particular types of case.

The time taken to prepare a report is an important issue. Magistrates frequently maintain that out-patient clinics are often unable to offer an appointment within the three weeks it will take to obtain a report in custody. In the London area there may have been, and may still occasionally be, some validity in this complaint. But when the Cambridge study of sexual offenders (Radzinowicz, 1957) noted in 1950 that 'in areas outside the metropolis and large cities, it was frequently difficult to obtain a medical report unless the offender was remanded in custody', they described a situation which no longer applies at least as far as Wessex is concerned.

Our study revealed that, in 107 bail cases about which there was sufficient information about the date of remand and the date of examination on bail, 13 (12 per cent) were seen within eight days of court request, 33 (31 per cent) within 15 days, 35 (33 per cent) within 22 days, and 11 (10 per cent) within 29 days. Only 5 (5 per cent) waited longer than four weeks before a psychiatric interview could be arranged, and the remaining ten appeared to have been examined by the psychiatrist before the court request. Our information did not suggest that an interview could not normally be arranged within four weeks, though of course a single interview may not be enough if further investigations (e.g. X-ray or EEG studies) are needed.

Where bail cases were interviewed. The geographical location of the hospital or clinic in relation to the magistrates' court may be important if, for example, a possibly subnormal person has to find his way to a hospital some miles away for examination. Among our sample the interviews took place in 19 hospitals and clinics, including the six principal hospitals to which the consultants were attached.

The development of facilities for out-patient treatment and examination of the mentally ill (largely arising from the fact that psychotropic drugs enable the majority to be maintained in the community), and the subsequent opening of psychiatric clinics in most large towns, sometimes in special centres, more often in the local general hospitals, served by consultants from the mental hospitals has made close liaison with local courts increasingly possible.

There are, occasionally, difficulties in the larger cities where out-patient clinics are held frequently, consultants may each have twenty or more patients to see in an afternoon, new, old and follow-up cases after hospital treatment. To give $1-1\frac{1}{2}$ hours to the examination of an offender is difficult and many psychiatrists considered that offenders should not be able to 'jump the queue' of new cases referred by general practitioners. In some towns the clinic may only be held on one afternoon a week or a fortnight; examination in three weeks may then be difficult.

Many consultants, however, told us that they could usually arrange to see an offender on another occasion at the hospital when they had more time and no doubt the Statutory Instrument 1967 (No. 1776 Witnesses Allowances)[1] which entitled them to a fee of about 8 guineas for a report, was intended to add some recompense for such extra work. We found, incidentally, that many consultants did not know they were entitled to a fee, or, if they did, how to obtain it.

Time Spent in Preparing Reports

The time taken with a forensic case may be important in relation to future developments. The consultants were asked in the questionnaire to state how long it took them to see the case, including travelling time.

Most bail cases would not have involved travelling, since offenders would usually come to the doctor. In the 118 cases in which this section was completed the answer probably referred to the interview itself. Nearly two-thirds of the medical remands on bail are dealt with in an hour or less; a further quarter take two hours or less and only 8 per cent took over two hours. Only six cases were interviewed on two or more occasions.

The time taken to see cases in custody, which in many cases may involve over an hour in both directions must influence the proportion of cases receiving treatment as out-patients on probation under Section 4. In Section 60 cases the need for hospital treatment may be quite clear to the prison medical officer, and the consultant who is called to see the offender and sign the order is very likely to agree. When the issue is whether an offender needs or is likely to benefit from treatment as an outpatient on probation, a difference of opinion is more likely and the officer will hesitate to call upon a consultant, especially from a considerable distance. If the consultant sees the offender on bail he makes his own decision at once. On this aspect of travelling time we unfortunately have no information.

[1] Under Section 32/3, Criminal Justice Act, 1967.

The Work of Prison Medical Officers

The preparation of medical reports on prisoners remanded in custody plays a larger part in the work of the prison medical officers if they work in a local prison. They have also to treat sick prisoners under sentence, as well as prepare reports for internal use, e.g. for parole, or recommendations for transfer etc. In the present survey we were concerned only with reports written for magistrates' courts in the Wessex Regional Hospital Board area. Prison medical officers had to prepare other reports, for the high courts in the area and magistrates' courts outside the area.

The persons remanded in Wessex in custody were seen in one of six prisons or remand centres, according to age, sex and location of the court: Winchester prison and remand centre 128; Dorchester prison 34; Exeter remand centre 4; Holloway 15; Pucklechurch remand centre 2.

For the Wessex sample TABLE 20 shows the distribution of reports by prison medical officers, equivalent to that shown in Table 19 for Health Service consultants.

Bearing in mind that a small number of consultant psychiatrists saw a substantial number of bail cases, we can say that for all the medical remands in the region, on bail or in custody, 54 per cent were reported upon by six doctors or 62 per cent by only nine doctors out of the 47 who were occasionally involved.

TABLE 20

NUMBER OF MEDICAL REPORTS IN CUSTODY
SUBMITTED BY PRISON MEDICAL OFFICERS
IN 8 MONTHS

No. of Reports	No. of Prison MOs	Total No. of Reports
1–2	7	12
3–5	3	11
27–34	5	160
No information		4
	15	187

As already mentioned, any one medical remand may be seen by several psychiatrists. The prison medical officer may, of course, consult a senior colleague, or a visiting consultant psychotherapist may be asked for his opinion. If a hospital order (Section 60) is made two doctors must examine the patient, and in psychiatric probation orders (Section 4 Criminal Justice Act) a second doctor outside prison must at least agree to treat the patient, usually after an examination. Of the male custodial remands in Wessex there was evidence that a second opinion by a hospital consultant was given in at least twelve cases apart from those receiving orders under Section 60 or Section 4.

Two doctors will also be concerned if there are two types of medical remand. In four cases a post-trial medical remand in custody was followed up by a further medical remand on bail. This is apt to occur if the prison medical officer feels that a Section 4 order would be useful but has not had time to secure the agreement of a consultant. There were also three cases of medical remand on bail, followed by a second medical remand in custody. Sometimes an accused person (or his counsel) will arrange for a report by another doctor for defence purposes. This is usual, for example, in murder cases. Reports for the defence are considered later.

CHAPTER VI

PHYSICAL AND MENTAL HEALTH AND CRIMINAL RECORD

THE best method of obtaining medical information posed many problems. The reports to court have a specific purpose and mention symptoms and patterns of reaction only if relevant to the recommendation; the level of intelligence, for example, will be mentioned only if it strongly affects the issue. To design a suitable questionnaire to overcome the difficulty was far from easy. Existing 'standardized' psychiatric interview schedules call for a good deal of preliminary discussion and training in interpretation, and are in any case not yet available for personality disorders. Our questionnaire (see APPENDIX 2) had to be filled in by over 40 different doctors with no explanation apart from a short 'glossary'. It had to be both short enough not to irritate busy practitioners and clearly relevant to the issues which they would naturally have in mind. Forensic interviews are more complicated than others since the patient's co-operation is not certain and in assessing behaviour disorders one often has to deduce personality characteristics from the history and recurrent patterns as well as from the demeanour of the patient.

The questionnaire was shown to half a dozen prison medical officers in Brixton prison, and revised in response to their difficulties or doubts. A space at the end was left for free observations by the doctor. We have no means of knowing how comparable are their standards of assessment (e.g. of slight, moderate, or severe ratings) or whether they are using the terms in a similar way. They are, however, the doctors who normally report to the courts.

PHYSICAL HEALTH

The doctors were asked whether the offender regarded physical ill health or disability as a problem, and how they assessed the situation. TABLE 21 shows that just under 20 per cent of males and 30 per cent of females felt that this was a problem to a greater or less degree, whereas the doctors considered that this was so in 15 per cent of males, and in 32 per cent of the females; that is, males tended to over-estimate, women to under-estimate, their disability in the doctor's view. However, there was an 85 per cent agreement between the two scales for men and 81 per cent for women. A wide range of problems was mentioned from alcohol to drugs to respiratory and other organic complaints.

This is one of the few topics on which some direct comparison can be made between the assessments by the doctors *and* those by the probation officers, for male medical remands and a control group.

TABLE 21
DOES THE SUBJECT AND THE DOCTOR REGARD PHYSICAL ILL HEALTH OR DISABILITY A PROBLEM?

| | Males | | Females | |
	No.	%	No.	%
Very much so	15 (9)	5·9 (3·5)	5 (6)	11·6 (14·0)
Slightly	34 (29)	13·3 (11·3)	8 (8)	18·6 (18·6)
Not at all	194 (206)	75·8 (80·5)	30 (29)	69·8 (67·4)
Don't know*	3 (3)	1·2 (1·2)	—	—
No information	10 (9)	3·9 (3·5)	—	—
Total	256 (256)	100 (100)	43 (43)	100 (100)

Figures in brackets represent the doctors' assessment.

* Throughout this chapter, the responses 'don't know' mean that the doctor marked this specific item on the questionnaire, whereas 'no information' means that all the items were left blank.

The main interest of the table is that the 'controls' show a degree of disability very similar to that of the medical remands. As the probation officers' assessment of the medical remands corresponds closely to that of the doctors (though a little more willing to allow complaints of 'slight' disability) suggests that their assessment is not wide of the mark.

TABLE 22
PROBATION OFFICERS' ESTIMATES: IS PHYSICAL ILL HEALTH OR DISABILITY A PROBLEM?

| | Male Medical Remands | | Control Group | |
	No.	%	No.	%
Very much so	10	8·8	8	7·0
Slightly	24	21·1	20	17·5
Not at all	70	61·4	81	71·1
Don't know	6	5·3	4	3·5
No information	4	3·5	1	0·9
	114	100	114	100

To return to the doctors' questionnaire, the remands were asked whether they had been in contact with a general hospital within one year, or within five years, or longer. Of the men, 9 per cent had been in contact in the last year, and a further 9 per cent in the last five years; but among the women 20 per cent had been in contact in the last year and 7 per cent in the last five years. In the figures of recent troubles among the women gynaecological conditions were reported by 10 per cent.

PAST MENTAL HEALTH: CONTACT WITH PSYCHIATRIC HOSPITALS

There was greater evidence of recent contact with a psychiatric hospital than with a general hospital. Among the men 21 per cent, and 47 per cent of the women, had been in some contact with a psychiatric hospital in the last year, and a further 15 per cent of men and 14 per cent of women in the last five years (9 per cent and 7 per cent respectively over five years before).

When the figures are adjusted for those who had had contact with *both* general and psychiatric hospitals in the last year (9 men and 6 women) 24 per cent of males and 54 per cent of females had contact in the last year and a further 15 per cent of males and 14 per cent of women in the last five years.

Of the 54 men who had contact with a psychiatric hospital in the last year, only 15 had attended the particular hospital where the consultant worked who was submitting the report (29 of them in fact were remanded in custody and so were seen by someone else). The women differed in this; 12 out of the 20 had been in contact with the hospital at which the consultant who prepared the report worked. This difference between men and women is almost entirely explained by the higher proportion of women seen on bail.

Of 18 men currently in touch with the hospital eleven were in-patients at the time; eight were remanded on bail and three in custody. Being an out-patient, however, afforded no protection against custody; six of the seven men receiving out-patient treatment were remanded in custody. Among the women three of the five in-patients were bailed and three of the four out-patients.

The psychiatrists were not asked for information about previous psychiatric illness or symptoms. Fairly detailed information about the current state was thought more useful.

The relatively high rate of recent contact with a psychiatric hospital is influenced by the fact that probation officers in Wessex had a pre-trial interview in nearly all cases except the most trivial and would have elicited any history of mental breakdown. One of the main results of this study has been to emphasize the importance of adequate information reaching the courts in time. In a London court, a woman in-patient was arrested for shoplifting on a Saturday afternoon outing (a fairly frequent activity of women in-patients, it seems) and remanded to prison without the court ever being aware of her hospital status.

PRESENT MENTAL STATE

The main intention was to obtain a broad description of the mental state, first with regard to symptoms and recognized syndromes, an aspect which probably would be of major interest to consultant psychiatrists in the Health Service. Five dimensions were described, namely, anxiety state, depression, other neurotic symptoms, psychosis, and dementia. Each if present was to be rated as severe, moderate, mild, or absent (and if the question was not answered, we included 'not known'). This was calculated to commend itself to the large majority of the Health Service psychiatrists, who took the view that 'psychiatry has a place in the treatment of offenders provided they are ill'. It may measure the perceived need to intervene or offer treatment.

Although these dimensions may be the prime considerations of psychiatrists they provide a poor description of the range of personality disorders which are often the principal problems in offenders. A second descriptive classification, therefore, included 'Basic Personality or Life Style'. Qualities to be rated on a similar scale of severe, moderate, etc. were (1) Mental Retardation, (2) Immature Personality, (3) Character Deficiency, (4) Mood Swings.

In 20 cases, the first or symptomatic part of the current mental state was not filled in. These were deducted, leaving 279. In a further 31 cases one or other section was not filled in, presumably because it was felt that other sections dealt fully with the symptoms.

The ratings of severity for each symptom separately are given in APPENDIX 6. The main conclusion was that only a small minority of men had any 'severe' rating on any symptom (11 per cent); and only two women had a 'severe' rating and that for 'other neurotic symptoms'. The commonest severe rating referred to 'other neurotic symptoms': 5 per cent in both sexes.

As one would suppose, there is a tendency for a severe rating or a principal 'moderate' rating to dominate the clinical picture, with some degree of mixture of symptoms in the 'mild' ratings. The best impression of the clinical presentation is probably achieved by showing the proportions with a severe or moderate rating (TABLE 23).

TABLE 23
PROPORTIONS WITH 'SEVERE' OR 'MODERATE' RATING FOR
EACH ITEM OF PRESENT MENTAL STATE

	Males		Females	
	No.	%	No.	%
Psychosis	18	7·0	0	—
Anxiety State	23	9·0	8	18·6
Depression	16	6·3	7	16·3
Other neurotic symptoms	31	12·1	6	14·0
Dementia	1	0·4	1	2·3

As several 'severe' or 'moderate' symptoms could, theoretically, be combined in a single individual, TABLE 24 gives another form of analysis based on the most serious rating.

It will be seen that in terms of the presence and severity of any symptom

11 per cent of males and 5 per cent of females had a severe rating
19 per cent of males and 29 per cent of females had a moderate rating
29 per cent of males and 37 per cent of females had at least one mild rating
41 per cent of males and 29 per cent of females had no symptoms

Altogether 70 per cent of men and 66 per cent of women had mild or indeed no symptoms. There is no information about comparability of standards of assessment but one may reasonably assume that the more severe the symptoms the greater the likelihood of comparability.

TABLE 24

ANALYSIS OF MOST SERIOUS RATING FOR PRESENT MENTAL
STATE FOR EACH PATIENT

Most serious rating for each patient	Males No.	%	Females No.	%
Severe				
Psychosis	9	3·8	—	—
Anxiety state	3	1·3	—	—
Depression	1	0·4	—	—
Other neurotic symptoms	13	5·5	2	4·9
Dementia	—	—	—	—
Moderate				
Psychosis	6	2·5	—	—
Anxiety state	9	3·8	2	4·9
Depression	6	2·5	2	4·9
Other neurotic symptoms	14	5·9	2	4·9
Dementia	1	0·4	1	2·4
Mixed	10	4·2	5	12·1
Mild symptoms				
1–4 symptoms	69	29·0	15	36·6
Absent				
No symptoms at all	97	40·8	12	29·3
Total	238	100	41	100

One would expect Health Service consultants to examine offenders within the framework of the hospital population, and the prison medical officers in relation to the offender population. 'Other neurotic symptoms' was the most frequently used severe rating and the prison medical officers made the most frequent use of it (18 out of the 26 occasions when it was used). Some degree of anxiety and depression is to be expected in someone being prosecuted for an offence, and the forensic psychiatrist has to assess from the history and the range of the patient's attitudes how much to allow for the consequences of arrest. 'Other neurotic symptoms' may be a more satisfactory way of indicating something different from the simple consequences of arrest or conviction, especially if one is used to dealing with lay magistrates who will not be impressed by a finding of anxiety or depression. As the judge said when told a rapist was 'abnormal'—'So I should hope.'

BASIC PERSONALITY OR LIFE STYLE

This aspect of mental assessment though regarded as essential, presented even greater difficulties, because there is no general agreement about personality differences.[1] The two-fold division of symptoms and personality

[1] The psychiatric classification of offenders presents great difficulties, which have not been completely resolved in the International Classification of Diseases schedule of psychiatric disorder, which was not used here. It is fairly well adapted to the needs of psychiatrists in the Health Service dealing with patients who seek their help or manifestly require it, but it lacks detail with regard to gradations of severity, the relation of personality disorder to symptoms, and motivation or suitability for treatment. The ICD classification of pathological personality types includes a sub-type of 'Antisocial Personality' suitable for a hospital population; but

was thought appropriate for the consultant psychiatrists, most of whom on interview expressed the general view that psychiatrists had a place in the treatment of offenders who were 'ill' but could not be expected to treat 'personality disorders'; a small minority adding that psychiatrists could treat some personality disorders but that this would demand a staff ratio and special facilities which they did not possess. Some measure of the degree of 'personality disorder' was required but it was important not to annoy doctors by an elaborate questionnaire about personality with whose subdivisions they might not agree. Measurement by psychological tests was not possible.

Of these four (somewhat ill-assorted) categories, intelligence or mental retardation is clearly essential, since marked subnormality comes within the ambit of the psychiatrist. Immaturity, not mere youthfulness, in the sense of Warren's (1969, 1973) 'level of immaturity in interpersonal relations' is perhaps the most important dimension in delinquency. Mood swings or emotional instability are familiar to psychiatrists. Character deficiency was intended to include those of relatively normal temperament, personality and maturity in whom a moral quality such as dishonesty, especially if circumscribed, is largely a culturally or environmentally induced trait.

The questionnaire replies showed, as one might expect, that over twice as many were reported to have severe or moderate degrees of these personality disorders as was the case with symptoms. The full distribution is given in APPENDIX 7. A severe degree of disorder was reported in 22 per cent of men and 28 per cent of women, and in 5 per cent and 14 per cent respectively the severe disorder related to two categories. Moderate disorder was reported in 40 per cent of men and 37 per cent of women. Only 14 per cent of men and 7 per cent of women were thought to show no significant personality disorder. The excess of personality disorders among women offenders, and a rather lesser excess of formal psychiatric disorder, is also a regular finding.

TABLE 25 gives a contracted version of the results. A double categorization was also made more frequently since mental retardation can co-exist with any of the other three. The concepts of immaturity and character deficiency almost certainly overlapped and even a very full and specific glossary might well have been resisted by the various views of over forty psychiatrists. Psychoanalytic classification, for example, tends to describe psychopathic states as 'character neurosis'. There was probably much more comparability in the assessment of personality disorder as severe, moderate, or slight.

Mental retardation is probably the most independent and universally defined category. As APPENDIX 7 shows it was assessed as severe in 2 per cent of males and 2 per cent of females and moderate in a further 5 per cent

---

liable to very uncertain use among a population of offenders, and used by 40 psychiatrists from widely different backgrounds, with whom we did not have persistent contact or discussion. There is no claim that the questionnaires used did not present many difficulties and uncertainties.

TABLE 25

ANALYSIS OF THE MOST SERIOUS RATING FOR BASIC
PERSONALITY OR LIFE STYLE FOR EACH PATIENT

Most serious rating for each patient	Males		Females	
	No.	%	No.	%
Severe				
Mental retardation	5	2·1	—	—
Immature personality	23	9·5	2	4·7
Character deficiency	12	5·0	3	7·0
Mood swings	2	0·8	1	2·3
Two disorders	13	5·3	6	13·9
Moderate				
Mental retardation	7	2·9	2	4·7
Immature personality	26	10·7	2	4·7
Character deficiency	25	10·3	3	7·0
Mood swings	7	2·9	—	—
Two disorders	33	13·7	9	21·0
Mild disorders				
1–4 disorders	54	22·3	12	27·9
Absent				
No disorder at all	35	14·5	3	7·0
Total	242	100·0	43	100·0

N.B. 14 questionnaires (all males) where there was no response made by psychiatrist to any of the items have been disregarded in this analysis.

and 14 per cent respectively. 'Severe' retardation does not, of course, imply severe subnormality in the sense of the Mental Health Act.

TABLE 26 combines the assessment of both psychiatric and personality disorder, showing that 28 per cent of men and 33 per cent of women were considered to be severely disordered in one or both respects. In 66 per cent

TABLE 26

MENTAL HEALTH SUMMARY SCALE

	Males		Females	
	No.	%	No.	%
Severe personality problems	32	12·5	6	14·0
Severe mental illness	4	1·6	1	2·3
Severe mental illness and moderate personality	12	4·7	1	2·3
Severe personality and moderate mental illness	14	5·5	6	14·0
Severe personality and severe mental illness	9	3·5	—	
Mild problems only	59	23·0	12	27·9
Moderate personality problem	65	25·4	12	27·9
Moderate mental illness	9	3·5	2	4·6
Moderate personality and moderate mental illness	21	8·2	3	7·0
No problems	19	7·4	—	—
No information	12	4·7	—	—
Total	256	100·0	43	100·0

of men and 77 per cent of women the severe and moderate ratings of the two categories of personality problems and mental illness did not overlap and in the categories where overlap did occur, in 14 per cent of men and 16 per cent of women, one or other of the groups was rated as severe. About a third of the men and a quarter of the women had minor or no mental health problems.

PHYSICAL AND MENTAL HEALTH

A good deal of attention has been given in recent years to the relationship between mental and physical ill health. In our present group there was no indication of close association or overlap; rather the reverse. With nine men and six women physical ill health or disability was 'very much' a problem, and 29 men and 8 women had 'slight' physical problems. Of the 9 men with serious physical disability, 5 had mild personality or psychiatric problems, moderate illness or personality disorder, and 5 of the 6 women with severe physical problems were in these mild grades. Only one man and one woman had both severe physical and mental problems. Of the 29 men with slight physical disability, 21 were in the milder mental categories and 5 of the 8 women. The medical reports had probably been requested because of mental *or* physical disability and the overlap was slight.

ALCOHOLIC AND DRUG ADDICTION

The rate of excessive drinking is high among offenders, especially among recidivists. In a stratified sample of the prison population in London, taking account of those serving the first sentence as well as recidivists, Gibbens and Silberman (1970) found that 40 per cent were excessive drinkers; the proportion rose to 50 per cent among those who had six or more previous prison sentences. TABLE 27 shows that in the present remanded population a

TABLE 27

ESTIMATE OF ALCOHOL ABUSE ACCORDING TO RATING OF PSYCHIATRIST

Use of Alcohol	Males No.	%	Females No.	%
Chronic alcoholic	20	7·8	5	11·6
Repeated drinker	48	18·8	6	14·0
No serious problem	168	65·6	32	74·4
No information	20	7·8	—	—
Total	256	100·0	43	100·0

quarter of both men and women were regarded as either chronic alcoholics or repeated drinkers.

Of the 25 men and women classified by the psychiatrists as chronic alcoholics, only two (men) had *not* apparently been drinking at the time of offence. Drunkenness at the time was also mentioned with regard to at least 22 of the repeated drinkers and 11 of these in the 'no serious problem' or 'no information' groups, but this question was often not answered.

All the chronic alcoholics were over 21 years of age and all but three (all males) were over thirty. Among the males over 30 in the sample, 17 (18·3 per cent) were rated as chronic alcoholics, and 20 (21·5 per cent) as repeated drinkers. Of the females over 30, exactly half were rated as chronic alcoholics (5 cases) or repeated drinkers (3 cases).

Among the men 25 per cent of the chronic alcoholics were rated as having severe mental or personality disorders; though these constituted only 7 per cent of men in these categories. A third were rated as having mild or no problems. Among those with mild, moderate, or no mental health or personality problems, 26 per cent were chronic alcoholics or repeated drinkers, which may have influenced their selection for remand.

The females had a higher incidence of chronic alcoholism. None were regarded as having no other problems and 21 per cent of those with severe personality or mental health problems were also rated as chronic alcoholic.

DRUG ABUSE

After attempts to derive adequate 'closed' questions for the questionnaire the issue was left partly open-ended, the psychiatrist being asked first to assess whether the patient was a 'user of drugs' (for non-medical purposes) and then to state, if appropriate, the kind of drug that was being used, and the degree of addiction.

TABLE 28
ESTIMATE OF DRUG ABUSE

Drugs—Degree of Use	Males		Females	
	No.	%	No.	%
Addicted	7	2·7	1	2·3
Regular	12	4·7	5	11·6
Intermittent	30	11·7	7	16·3
Non-user	184	71·9	28	65·1
No information	23	9·0	2	4·7
Total	256	100·0	43	100·0

A higher proportion were rated as non-users—72 per cent men and 65 per cent women—than with alcohol. If the criterion had been broader (as with alcohol), for example 'no serious drug problem', it would probably have been higher still.

Among the 62 cases reported, the type of drug was not mentioned (or no special drug) in 13 cases. Of the 49 remaining, cannabis was used (predominately intermittently) by 15, LSD by 12, and heroin by a further 8 (at least three of whom were classed as addicted). The remainder used, in varying degrees, amphetamine or barbiturates; a further 25 men and women were described as regular or addicted drug users.

Younger rather than older groups were involved. Of the males, 29 were between 17 and 20 (of whom two were addicted), 18 between 21 and 29 (five addicted) and two (both intermittent users) were over 30. No females were in the age group 21 to 29; eight were under 21 (one addicted) and the other five over thirty.

In respect of mental or personality disorder, drug users were much more often assessed as being seriously disordered than alcoholics. None of the 25 men and women was regarded as having 'no problems' and in only two men were these considered 'mild'; seven men and women were rated as having severe personality disorders with or without added mental illness.

'No Abnormality'

In 19 men (6 per cent) no symptoms or personality disorders were reported, but one had a physical ill health problem, eight were repeated or excessive drinkers, two abused drugs to some degree. Of the remaining eight, reported to be normal mentally, physically and in personality, two had had previous mental illnesses (one a schizophrenic breakdown who was offered treatment if there was a recurrence); three were sexual deviants (one hypersexual, one a repeated exhibitionist and one described as normal). One was 'normal apart from a tendency to steal cars' and two were 'normal' with no elaboration.

The relation of mental or personality disorder to the sentence is laid out in APPENDIX 8. This will be considered in more detail after the social and criminal history of the remands, which give a clearer picture of the type of population. Of those males rated as severely disordered in one or both respects 31 per cent received a medical disposal, and 46 per cent received a non-custodial and 17 per cent a custodial sentence. Among the women 64 per cent of those receiving non-custodial sentences were rated as severely disordered.

Criminal Record

The bald description of symptoms and types of personality disorder does not provide a very human picture of the remands. In CHAPTER VIII dealing with the social circumstances of a controlled sample, a more rounded picture will emerge, but the full criminal record of the remands was obtained independently and helped to fill in the picture. No information was obtained about 13 males and 5 females.

Very trivial offences can lead to a court appearance—and indeed to a medical remand—but in considering the previous criminal history of offenders one must recognize the limitation of sources of information. Some minor offences, such as drunkenness, are not systematically recorded by the criminal record office, though they may involve just as elaborate court proceedings. Acquittals, or committals to hospital under Section 60 (2) of the Mental Health Act of 1959 (i.e. without recording a conviction) will also not be recorded. The present analysis, therefore, deals with 'standard list' offences, which are usually fully recorded, though in certain instances we have considered other offences when known.

As many as 20 per cent of men and 27 per cent of women were thus first offenders in relation to both adult and juvenile offences.

There was a remarkable lack of previous juvenile offences among the remands, 66 per cent of males and 80 per cent of females had none recorded. 10 per cent of males and no females had three or more juvenile findings of guilt. Absolute reliance cannot be placed on this result, especially with older adults with many subsequent convictions when juvenile offences tend to fade into relative insignificance. About 30 per cent of the remands were in this older recidivist category, but this cannot account entirely for the low figures on a juvenile record.

TABLE 29 (B) shows previous *adult* convictions. The great majority of both sexes had previous convictions; nearly one in five had six or more convictions. The high proportion of women with previous adult convictions—a third with three or more—is striking, as normally the overwhelming majority of women coming before the courts are first or, at most, second offenders. Those remanded for a medical report are clearly a very disordered group.

TABLE 29 (C) shows the distribution of age at first conviction as a typical curve of criminality declining with age among males, though with a bias towards late onset in the men. In the general offender population far less than (as here) one-fifth of male offenders are first convicted at 30 or over. The distribution for females follows the common pattern, i.e. a peak age at 17–20 (since so many are in need of care or control before 17), and a resurgence, due very largely to shoplifting, between 30–39—a phenomenon unique in the criminal world.

The length of criminal career from first to most recent conviction gives another indication of chronicity (TABLE 29 (D)). Some 47 per cent of men and 31 per cent of women had a career of five years or more. Sellin (1958) showed many years ago that the criminal career of more serious offenders tends to last about this time, but in the present series the criminal career went on much longer for nearly a quarter in each sex. The overwhelming majority of previous offences were property offences in some form. Violence to the person (indictable or non-indictable) (15 per cent of men) was low in view of the high rate of alcoholism, for the two usually go together, and the proportion among women was similar (14 per cent). Sexual offences against males and females were in the record of 17 per cent of the men but of only one woman.

TABLE 29 (E) (Previous Sentences) shows that over half were already known to the probation service. A substantial proportion of both sexes had several previous prison sentences, and most have presented serious problems. The relatively high proportion who had had previous psychiatric treatment orders through the courts either on probation or in hospital is especially interesting.

TABLE 29

CRIMINAL HISTORY OF WESSEX (1970–1 SAMPLE)

(A) TOTAL COURT APPEARANCES
(Adult and Juvenile)

	Males %	Females %
Nil	19·7	27·4
1–2	31·1	37·3
3–5	25·9	17·7
6–9	12·4	13·7
10–20+	11·0	3·9
	100·0	100·0
	(274)	(51)

(B) PREVIOUS ADULT CONVICTIONS

	Males %	Females %
Nil	28·1	31·4
1–2	32·9	33·3
3–5	20·8	21·5
6–9	9·1	9·8
10–20+	9·1	3·9
	100·0	100·0
	(274)	(51)

(C) AGE AT FIRST CONVICTION

	Males %	Females %
8–16	35·1	19·6
17–20	26·6	37·3
21–9	19·4	15·6
30–9	10·2	21·6
40+	8·0	5·9
NK	0·7	—
	100·0	100·0
	(274)	(51)

(D) LENGTH OF CRIMINAL CAREER

	Males %	Females %
No previous	19·3	27·5
Up to 3 yrs.	23·0	29·5
Up to 10 yrs.	34·3	19·5
Over 10 yrs.	23·3	23·5
	100·0	100·0
	(274)	(51)

(E) PREVIOUS SENTENCES

	Males %	Females %
Probation Order	54	55
Borstal Sentence	11	6
Prison Sentences of up to 3 months:		
1–3 times	11	6
4 or more times	6	2
Prison Sentences of over 3 months:		
1–3 times	17	8
4 or more times	8	4
Probation with condition of treatment	10	6
Previous Hospital Order S60	5·5	8
Total Number of Cases	274	51

N.B. Since some people had several types of sentences, figures do not add up to 100.

Approximately 20 per cent of men and 6 per cent of women had been released from their last custodial sentence in the last year; but 9 per cent of men and 6 per cent of women had passed over three years since their last custodial sentence. But the last custodial sentence was imprisonment in only 14 per cent of men and 2 per cent of women.

CHAPTER VII

DOCTORS' VIEWS ON THE REMAND PROCEDURE

THE doctors were asked a number of questions about the practical aspects of reporting.

PRESUMED REASONS FOR THE REMAND

There are at least three parties to the medical reports, each with a different viewpoint, the magistrate who requests it, the offender who submits to it, and the doctor who supplies it. Others may initiate a request: defending counsel or solicitor, probation officer, sometimes the offender himself or his relatives. Each party has different expectations and motives and there are complicated problems of communication.

Under Rule 43 of the Magistrates' Courts Rules, 1968, a 'statement of the reason why the court is of the opinion that an inquiry ought to be made into his physical or mental condition and of any information before the court about his physical or mental condition should be completed and made available to the medical officer involved'. A preliminary investigation showed that this document was unlikely to be of much use for research purposes. Some courts completed the form conscientiously and provided a full picture of what led the court to ask the question. Other courts provided vague generalisations (e.g. 'NFA', 'no fixed abode'). *In 44 per cent of cases this document did not appear to have been forwarded at all.* Sometimes the probation officer's report, accompanying the request for an appointment, will provide a full social and criminal history and an account of what was in the court's mind; but sometimes the probation officer is not in court at the time.

The most obvious way to find out why a person was remanded is to ask the magistrates. Dr. Peter Scott (1967) profitably used this approach with magistrates in juvenile court cases who agreed to 'record their reasons for remanding boys in custody', but this was on a small scale and we did not think it practicable to circulate a request of this kind to several hundreds of magistrates in Wessex. More important, this might have led to a subtle alteration in practice by drawing attention to the study and we were anxious to study the on-going procedures without risk of influencing them.

From experience we know that psychiatrists, especially prison medical officers, who have the greatest experience, often wonder why an offender has been remanded for a medical report. Often the nature of the offence raises the question of whether psychological treatment would be helpful—especially sex offences, and some offences involving unexplained violence or drug taking. But doctors may not realize that in other cases the court may not consider there to be any psychiatric condition, but wishes to make sure before passing the sentence of imprisonment that seems to be required. Sometimes, for example, with chronic alcoholic petty recidivists, they may be baffled about what to do for the best, and hope that a psychiatrist may be able to make a constructive suggestion. But there are probably more routine reasons.

The doctors were asked whether any of five reasons was, in their view, the main one; but they were asked in an open-ended question to say what other reasons were regarded as probable. The replies, some of which fall into more than one category, were as follows:

TABLE 30
DOCTORS' VIEWS ON WHY MEDICAL REMAND WAS REQUIRED

| | *Males* | | *Females* | |
Possible reasons	*No.*	*%*	*No.*	*%*
Patient appeared ill in court	9	3·5	2	4·7
Court knew of or suspected previous mental illness	84	34·4	27	62·8
Nature of present offence	90	35·2	9	20·9
Medical inquiry added to others for good measure	27	10·6	3	7·0
Court felt a taste of prison would act as a warning	6	2·3	1	2·3
Probation officer's request*	30	11·7	4	9·3
Solicitor's or relatives' request*	4	1·6	—	—
Other or not answered	21	8·2	—	—

* The reason, if possible, was fitted into the first five categories. These referred to some additional stated reasons.

The nature of the present offence (35 per cent) and previous knowledge or suspicion of mental ill health (34 per cent) accounted for the great majority; the latter was overwhelmingly important among the women. 'A taste of prison as a warning' of course only applied to custodial remands. The 'nature of the offence' often referred to those committing sex offences, which applied to 36 per cent of those in this category. In the 'nature of offence' category only four of the nine women were shoplifters. Apart from the possible use of custody as a warning in a few cases, and some reports requested for 'good measure' in addition to, for example, suitability for Borstal reports, the suggested reason did not appear to influence the choice of custody or bail to any great extent.

The doctors thought the requests for a medical report reasonable in 76 per cent of men and 86 per cent of women, unreasonable in 12 per cent of men and 7 per cent of women; they were undecided about 8 per cent and 2 per cent respectively. In the category of 'adding a medical report for good measure', it was thought to be reasonable in 45 per cent. In 97 per cent of the male 'unreasonable' cases, the remand had been in custody; they amounted to 18 per cent of all the custodial remands, so that the prison medical officer apparently considered nearly one in five of reports to be unnecessary. Such a view would vary according to whether the psychiatrist saw his role as limited to the detection of frank mental illness, or as a wider one of contributing to the understanding and management of the offender. As an official medical adviser to the court, the prison medical officer, in the past at least, has usually been advised to restrict his comments to medical aspects, and not include comments upon likely response to different sorts of penal treatment, which might be misused by defence or prosecution or seen as attempting to influence the court. The consultant psychiatrist in the health service is in this respect his own master.

INTERVIEW DEMEANOUR OF THE PATIENT

Martin Davies (1969) in his study of the attitudes of probationers at the beginning of a probation order, observed that 'in probation, it might be expected that the clientele would include a large number who felt suspicious or possibly resentful of their position and, in order to check on this, probation officers were asked whether the probationers had shown any signs of sullenness, hostility, friendliness, or willingness to discuss their problem'. Similarly (but following Davies' advice, anxiety was added to the list) psychiatrists were asked to consider whether the persons medically remanded showed any such signs.

The present sample was not really comparable with the much younger offenders discussed in Davies' survey of probation: a much *lower* proportion in our sample were considered sullen or hostile, and a lower proportion were rated as friendly. A higher proportion were willing to discuss their problems.

The results were interesting, especially when responses were considered for bail or custody cases separately, as shown in TABLE 31. The figures have to be set out in some detail.

The differences, though not large, show a systematic tendency. Contrary to expectation, a higher proportion of men remanded on bail were rated as sullen, hostile, but anxious and less friendly; more willing, however, to discuss their problems. The women, however, were rated on bail as much less hostile, somewhat less sullen, more anxious and friendly and willing to discuss their problems.

These results, though open to a number of interpretations, touch upon issues which are probably of great importance. Does the difference lie in the doctors or in the offenders, or more probably, both? A consultant psychiatrist in the Health Service is used to seeing highly co-operative patients who have voluntarily sought his help; the more cautious, reserved, and perhaps suspicious offender may seem very different. The woman offender, however, is more likely to seem alarmed and to appeal for help to the psychiatrist, especially if he is a man; when in custody the recidivist woman offender, as many of these were, is often angry, irritable or alarmed

TABLE 31

PSYCHIATRISTS' ASSESSMENT OF THE DEFENDANT'S
INTERVIEW DEMEANOUR CONSIDERED IN TERMS OF THE TYPE
OF MEDICAL REMAND

| | Type of Medical Remand | | | |
| | Males | | Females | |
	Remanded in custody %	Remanded on bail %	Remanded in custody %	Remanded on bail %
Sullenness—Yes	6·1	13·2	21·4	20·7
No	88·5	79·1	57·2	69·0
No information	5·4	7·7	21·4	10·3
Total	(165)	(91)	(14)	(29)
Hostility—Yes	8·5	11·0	14·3	6·9
No	86·1	80·2	71·4	82·8
No information	5·4	8·8	14·3	10·3
Total	(165)	(91)	(14)	(29)
Friendliness—Yes	71·5	67·0	64·3	69·0
No	23·0	20·9	28·6	24·1
No information	5·5	12·1	7·1	6·9
Total	(165)	(91)	(14)	(29)
Anxiety—Yes	36·4	41·8	57·1	65·5
No	59·4	48·3	28·6	27·6
No information	4·2	9·9	14·3	6·9
Total	(165)	(91)	(14)	(29)
Willingness to discuss problems—				
Yes	81·2	85·7	85·8	89·6
No	14·5	9·9	7·1	6·9
No information	4·3	4·4	7·1	3·5
Total	(165)	(91)	(14)	(29)

showing much more violence to staff and other inmates than do male offenders; men in prison frequently resign themselves to the strict discipline and fall into the pattern of institutional life, tending to regard the doctor as a useful ally. There is no doubt a difference in type both of doctor and offender, but the result clearly highlights the problem of whether one obtains a truer picture of basic characteristics during an interview in custody, or on bail.

DIFFICULTIES IN COMPLETING THE REPORT

The above variation in co-operativeness of offenders may account for some of the difficulties in assessment. In seven cases the psychiatrist specifically mentioned that the offender's attitude had caused such difficulties, varying from 'professed amnesia', or 'no co-operation whatsoever' to being 'conned by a blandly lying adolescent'.

Several other practical difficulties emerged: (1) in 10 cases, 8 seen in prison, *social reports or hospital records of previous treatment were lacking.* (2) Difficulty in obtaining a *psychological test report* was mentioned in 11 cases, eight on bail (involving four consultants). In remand homes and remand centres there are facilities for routine testing, but in hospitals for adults (even hospitals for subnormals) or prisons, special arrangements have to be made for psychological examination, which may be difficult to arrange at an outpatient visit without prior notice. Moreover, to test and interview the offender in one session runs the risk of fatiguing him unduly. There may not be time to organize a second visit. (3) Lack of time to arrange an interview or lack of information about the reasons for the court's request were mentioned on a few occasions. (4) Availability and usefulness or otherwise of the probation officer's report (see TABLE 32).

TABLE 32

ASSESSMENT BY PSYCHIATRISTS WHETHER THE PROBATION REPORT WAS USEFUL

Was the probation report useful?	Males		Females	
	No.	%	No.	%
Yes	157	61·4	26	60·5
No	22	8·6	1	2·3
Not seen	59	23·0	15	34·9
No information	18	7·0	1	2·3
Total	256	100·0	43	100·0

The reference to some reports not being useful may mean that they did not contribute more than the doctor had obtained himself from the offender or relatives. With chronic recidivists, especially vagrants or those living rough, the probation officer may have little to contribute except a few confused details provided by the offender; such cases are sometimes remanded in custody at once without perhaps the knowledge of the officer until later. (5) Out-patient suitability. The doctors were asked to rate the offender's suitability for out-patient treatment. There were three reasons for this: (a) Whether or not psychiatric treatment was advised, the reliability was of interest. (b) This was especially so in relation to the use of bail, as, if reliable, most offenders—except for very serious offences—should have been suitable for a medical report on bail. (c) The relationship of suitability to personality diagnosis was of interest.

Of 41 offenders who received a probation order with a condition of mental treatment three had been assessed as 'definitely unreliable'. In the unreliable category were five who received in-patient treatment and 10 (48 per cent) of those who were given hospital orders.

There was only a very moderate relationship between 'reliability' and severity of mental or personality disorder—27 per cent of the 'very reliable', 40 per cent of the 'fairly reliable' and 60 per cent of the 'definitely unreliable' were severely disordered. The women on the whole tended to be regarded as less reliable than the men, only 12 per cent being regarded as very reliable.

There was a closer relationship between remand on bail and reliability; 22 per cent of those bailed were 'very reliable' compared with 8 per cent of those in custody; 24 per cent of the bailed were 'definitely unreliable' compared with 45 per cent of those in custody. Among the women four of the five 'very reliable' were bailed but over half (55 per cent) of all the bailed women were regarded as 'definitely unreliable'. The Holloway prison medical officers possibly took a moderate view for the majority of custody cases (57 per cent) were judged 'fairly reliable' and only 35 per cent 'definitely unreliable'.

TABLE 33

PSYCHIATRISTS' ASSESSMENT OF OUT-PATIENT SUITABILITY

	Males		Females	
	No.	%	No.	%
Very reliable	33	12·9	5	11·7
Fairly reliable	92	35·9	17	39·5
Definitely unreliable	116	45·3	21	48·8
No information	15	5·9	—	—
Total	256	100·0	43	100·0

RECOMMENDATION TO THE COURT

Of all the men 26 per cent were recommended by the psychiatrist in the court report for medical treatment, either formal or informal as in-patients or out-patients. This is a high proportion compared with the London area, as earlier chapters suggest. Previous studies have suggested that courts follow the recommendation of the psychiatrist in the vast majority of cases. Sparks (1966) noted 'that the courts followed definite recommendations for mental treatment in 90 per cent of the cases in which recommendations were made'. Only one out of 73 recommendations for hospital orders was not acted upon: the defendant himself challenged the medical evidence (and was sentenced to 14 days' imprisonment). Some years earlier De Berker (1960) showed that courts follow 'special action' suggested by medical officers in 92 per cent of cases.

In the present sample a hospital order was recommended for 12 males and 5 females, and was acted upon for 11 of the 12 males[1] and all the females. The Mental Health Act categories were as follows

Mental illness	9 men
Psychopathic disorder	1 man
Subnormality	5 (2 men, 3 women)
Severe subnormality	1 woman
Category unknown	1 woman

[1] The twelfth was a 'severe chronic schizophrenic' who had received hospital treatment since 1952. After several remands on bail to his own hospital he was made subject to a Section 60 order in the end.

Four of the five female cases involved subnormality or severe subnormality.

A probation order with a condition of psychiatric treatment was recorded more frequently (35 males and 5 females). Of these, 9 who were recommended for in-patient treatment were made subject to such an order and 15 out-patient recommendations were followed, recommendations for treatment of this kind for men was followed in 69 per cent.[1]

Of the remaining 10 men for whom the recommendation was not followed, five were put on probation, two discharged, two fined, and one given a suspended sentence.

Informal psychiatric treatment was offered to an additional 25 men and 4 women: as out-patients to 15 men and 2 women, as in-patients to 6 men and 1 woman, in specialized drug or alcoholic unit to 4 males and 1 woman. Many psychiatrists view court orders with some suspicion, and a fear that they may have to account for their decisions or be hedged about by restrictions. More important, many consider that if a patient genuinely wishes for treatment, he will need no pressure or compulsion, and a court order will merely make it difficult to judge his sincerity and true motivation. In some forms of behavioural treatment of addiction to alcohol or drugs special importance is attached to motivation. Admission to a specialized unit may be limited to those who have successfully demonstrated their determination to participate actively in helping themselves and others, rather than a passive willingness to let doctors treat them. The doctors may consider that the threat of punishment implicit in a court appearance makes the assessment of true motivation more difficult.

The opinions of medical officers are probably more heavily influenced by the social and professional setting in which they work than they believe. All of the recommendations for treatment in prison and for 16 out of 17 institutional sentences were made by prison doctors. Of the recommendations for a supportive environment (hostels, sheltered communities, etc.) 71 per cent came from a hospital, i.e. community based psychiatrist. Although remands to custody or on bail were no doubt selectively distributed each group of doctors probably recommend treatment within their knowledge and experience. If so, the decision to remand on bail or in custody will in itself influence the options open to the court and, ultimately, the offender. In APPENDIX 8 we describe the relationship between medical disposals, non-custodial or custodial sentences in relation to the assessment of mental and personality disorders. It will be seen that these dimensions are to a fairly large extent independent of one another. Although the highest proportion (40 per cent) of those with non-custodial sentences are judged to have mild or no problems, this also applied to 33 per cent of those given custodial sentences and to 11 per cent of those given medical disposals. Similarly 23 per

---

[1] Analysis refers to cases on which we have relevant information; there were some who received a medical disposal but no questionnaire or medical report was returned.

cent of those given non-custodial sentences and 20 per cent of those given custodial sentences were rated as having 'severe' mental or personality problems; half the medical disposals, however, had 'severe' disorders. One would not, however, expect a very close relationship, for an individual criminal act does not necessarily have a close relationship to any mental or personality disorder.

CHAPTER VIII

CRIMINAL AND SOCIAL HISTORY OF A CONTROLLED SAMPLE

IT was planned that each man remanded should have a questionnaire completed by a doctor, another completed by the probation officer dealing with social aspects and other matters, and a third covering the 'next case aged 17 or over (not medically remanded) for whom the officer prepared a social inquiry'. As the great majority of offenders have a probation inquiry before trial in Wessex, the 'next case' would, it was hoped, provide a measure of the difference between medical remands and the general run of offenders coming before the courts, and at least some clues to the motives of the selection made by the courts.

A full quota of two questionnaires for each remand and one for a control was only completed in 40 per cent of cases, a rather low rate of response. It was not possible to visit all the probation officers in a large region to explain the purpose of the study, as was done with the much smaller number of psychiatrists. We did visit probation officers in the busiest urban centres where there are many medical remands, and more questionnaires were completed by them. In the three largest courts dealing with 35 male medical remands in the period, questionnaires were completed in 50 per cent; four medium sized courts (12–18 reports) returned 38 per cent; but 23 small courts (less than 10 remands) only returned 23 per cent. At one extreme, one court supplied completed forms in 85 per cent of cases; at the other, a court only completed 10 per cent. In small offices with few remands it was no doubt less easy to remember that a questionnaire on the next case was requested. Sometimes the next case was a high court case, or an offender was remanded after conviction with a social inquiry report not prepared by the officer or the officer would not know that at a later hearing a medical report had been requested.

So far as the medical remands are concerned the 114 completed questionnaires *are* representative—they do not differ significantly from the total 287 cases in any respect for which there is information, e.g. the age distribution, the type of offence, the proportion remanded in custody or on bail or the sentence. For the control group, however, this is not the case. The TABLE 34 comparison with the court turnover of all male indictable offenders who come before the Wessex courts—information which arrived many months after the analysis had been completed—shows, that in relation to age, perhaps the most important single fact about any offender, the controls are not closely representative, but are biased towards a group which is younger than average.

In what follows the differences between the two groups will have to be regarded as of uncertain significance. The experienced criminologist will see that some are almost certainly related mainly to age. But the purpose of the analysis was two-fold (*a*) to describe on the one hand the social characteristics of the remands and (*b*) the difference with a control group. The first of these intentions has been fulfilled; the remands *are* representative and, as will be seen, this is far the most important purpose.

TABLE 34
AGE DISTRIBUTION

Age Group	Male Medical		Control Group		Total Wessex Court Turnover (Indictable Offences)	
	No.	%	No.	%	No.	%
17–20	31	27·2	57	50·0	2,349	33·2
21–9	40	35·1	38	33·3	2,590	36·6
30+	43	37·7	19	16·7	2,137	30·2
Total	114	100·0	114	100·0	7,076	100·0

The information requested of the probation officers was intentionally restricted to straightforward questions that they could answer without difficulty or diverting too much time from their other duties. These questions referred to (1) Age. (2) Previous criminal record (we also obtained the official record on the medical remand sample which is probably fuller than the information which probation officers receive or at least record). (3) Regional origin. (4) Marital status. (5) Present accommodation and contact with relatives. (6) Employment. (7) Certain medical information. (8) Officers' views about the case.

Criminal Record. In a previous chapter we discussed the criminal records of the whole male medical remand sample of 287 cases. The differences in the comparison groups were clearly strongly influenced by the fact that half of the controls were aged 17–21. A significant excess of controls were first offenders, with neither previous convictions nor findings of guilt (26 per cent compared with 15 per cent) and significantly more had previous juvenile findings of guilt (45 per cent compared with 31 per cent). The medical remands, as one might suppose from their greater age, had a higher proportion of previous adult convictions (74 per cent compared with 53 per cent) than the controls. The medical remands contained a higher proportion with previous adult convictions but with no juvenile findings of guilt, and it was tempting to suppose that this might confirm the (probably quite correct) impression that the mentally disturbed offender is found more often among adults who have been law-abiding as juveniles but have encountered particular stresses in adult life. However, many of the medical remands were recidivists of over 30 and when there are many previous adult convictions the juvenile delinquent record is sometimes ignored in the list of previous offences. The medical remands had a marked excess with four or more adult convictions (34 per cent compared with 18 per cent). The controls, however, although younger included a fair number who were recidivists as adults—the proportion with one to two previous adult convictions was similar in both groups (39 per cent remands; 35 per cent controls).

Rapid failure after a custodial sentence might have led the courts to inquire more closely into the possible reasons. In fact, in spite of the age differences, there was little difference in the two groups in length of time since release from a previous custodial sentence (adult or juvenile); 54 per cent had no previous custodial experience, 11 per cent had offended within a year of release, 11 per cent less than three years, and 12 per cent more than three years: (not known, 4 per cent). Failure after a substantial period crime-free is perhaps as likely to stimulate close inquiry as rapid relapse.

One motive for a medical remand may be that the present offence is uncharacteristic or inconsistent, e.g. a thief who commits a sex offence. Probation officers were asked to assess whether the present offence was inconsistent with previous behaviour. It was considered to be so in 25 per cent both of remands *and* controls. When only those who had a previous conviction were considered, the present offence was regarded in fact as *more* often inconsistent in the controls.

Place of birth. About half of all the men were born in south or west England (slightly higher among the control group (56 per cent) than among the medical remands (45 per cent)). This difference though not statistically significant suggests that medical remands have a higher degree of mobility, and since 16 per cent of remands came from the Home Counties compared with 9 per cent of controls they may more often have been Londoners. Wessex is not a main reception area for those born outside the British Isles (only 3 per cent and 6 per cent) nor for Irish immigrants (3 per cent and 2 per cent), who in London reach about 15 per cent in the population and before the courts.

Place of birth does not, however, necessarily distinguish those who may have lived away from their place of birth for most of their lives. In both groups the majority had been resident in Wessex for three years or more— 54 per cent of remands and 72 per cent of controls. But there was a statistically significant (0·5 per cent level) excess of remands who had been in Wessex for less than a month (18 per cent compared with only 6 per cent of controls). Altogether one-third of remands had been in Wessex for less than a year compared with 18 per cent of controls. A larger number of controls were aged 17 to 20, and one would expect many of these to be in their own homes or living locally.

Marital Status. The marital history of offenders is often checkered and not always remembered accurately. We have limited our interest to the present situation at the time of the inquiry and any important changes in marital status occurring within the prevailing three years.

TABLE 35
MARITAL STATUS

Marital status	Male Medical Remands		Control Group	
	No.	%	No.	%
Single	69	60·5	72	63·2
Married or Cohabiting	20	17·5	30	26·3
Divorced/Separated/Widowed	24	21·1	12	10·5
No information	1	0·9	—	—
Total	114	100·0	114	100·0

Since half the controls are aged 17–20 it is surprising that an equally large proportion of the much older medical remands are single, and not cohabiting. This must almost certainly be an excess compared with the general non-offending population.

TABLE 36 gives further details of the period at which marriage and

TABLE 36
EVIDENCE OF BEING MARRIED OR COHABITING AT SOME STAGE

Evidence of being married or cohabiting at some stage	Male Medical Remands		Control Group	
	No.	%	No.	%
At Present Married/Cohabiting				
Married/Cohabiting (3 yrs. or more)	18	40·9	23	54·8
Married/Cohabiting (within last 3 yrs.)	2	4·5	7	16·7
Formerly Married				
Separated/Divorced (3 yrs. or more)	8	18·2	3	7·1
Separated/Divorced (within last 3 yrs.)	16*	36·4	9†	21·4
Total	44	100·0	42	100·0

* This includes one man who was widowed within the last three years as well as six men who were married *and* separated in that time.
† This figure includes two men who were married *and* separated within the last three years.

separation have occurred. The medical remands though older have a rather low rate of stable marriages for over three years and a high rate of separation and divorce in the present three years, which may of course have played a part in their present offence. Six in this group had married *and* separated within the last three years as had two of the nine controls in this category.

Accommodation and contact with close relatives. The medical remands were more often of 'no fixed abode' (23 per cent compared with 3 per cent of controls). Fewer were in a self-contained flat or house (44 per cent against 65 per cent). The proportions in this accommodation with wife (30 per cent), parents (54 per cent) or alone (10 per cent) with relatives or friends (5 per cent) were equal, as were those (about 22 per cent) in bedsitters, lodgings, or hostels (about 6 per cent).

Medical remands were undoubtedly more isolated socially: 40 per cent lived alone or slept rough (controls 20 per cent (significant at 0·5 per cent level)); 28 per cent had been at their present address for two years or more (controls 45 per cent); 24 per cent had no address at all (controls 3 per cent). Such factors probably play a large part in the decision to remand in custody or on bail and whether probation or custody is an appropriate sentence. Many offenders are remanded for reports with the unspoken question 'Can you suggest where this man might go ?' This isolation was also reflected in the proportion in weekly contact with a close relative. Medical remands frequently had 'no contact' (47 per cent compared with 22 per cent) and 37 per cent were in weekly contact with parents as compared with 52 per cent among controls (as one would expect of the younger group). Smaller, about equal, proportions were in contact mainly with siblings, children, or other close relatives.

Employment. The degree of current employment was poor in both groups— 66 per cent of the medical remands were unemployed, as compared with 46 per cent of controls (0·5 per cent significance) and 15 had not had employment for at least a year as compared with only one control. Among the remands who *were* employed, a higher proportion had been in work for a year or more (54 per cent compared with 33 per cent); there were 19 offenders in each group. In spite of the many young offenders there were only six students.

The employment record is difficult to categorize. A probation officer's general rating is probably as accurate as any method. Remands and controls did not differ markedly in the categories of 'regular' work (higher than labouring) (24 per cent; 31 per cent); 'regular' labouring or 'casual' work (16 per cent: 24 per cent) and 'some' work with spells of unemployment (37 per cent; 38 per cent); the outstanding difference was in 'mostly or totally unemployed', 22 per cent for remands compared with 4 per cent for controls.

Social Class. According to socio-economic group method of allocating social class the main difference was the higher proportion of controls in skilled (manual) class III M (14 per cent remands, 29 per cent controls) followed by a higher rate of remands in the next class 'partly skilled occupations' IV (25 per cent but 16 per cent controls).

The value of social background data lies largely in the information they give about the medical remands, who are certainly representative, rather than in the somewhat doubtful comparison with the controls.

Medical Questions. Probation officers' opinions about whether physical ill health or disability showed no difference between remands and controls;

'very much so' 9 per cent remands, 7 per cent controls; 'slightly' 21 per cent and 18 per cent. More controls had had contact with a general hospital in the last year, 17 per cent against 12 per cent, though fewer were in *current* contact. On the other hand contact with a psychiatric hospital in the last year was virtually confined to the medical remands (19 per cent compared with only one control): similarly with contact in the last five years (22 per cent against 2 per cent). No doubt this played a large part in probation officers' suggestions that a psychiatric report was advisable.

The officers were, like the psychiatrists, asked to judge the clients as very reliable (17 per cent, 17 per cent), fairly reliable (34 per cent, 40 per cent) or probably unreliable (46 per cent, 38 per cent) for out-patient treatment, if advised. The controls were judged to be marginally more reliable though this difference was not statistically significant.

The need for a medical report. The officer was asked to say in each case whether he felt a psychiatric report would be *useful*. TABLE 37 shows the results.

TABLE 37
USEFULNESS OF A MEDICAL REPORT

	Male Medical Remands		Control Group	
	No.	%	No.	%
Usefulness of Medical Report				
Definitely Yes	65	57·0	4	3·5
Probably Yes	38	33·3	21	18·4
Probably No	10	8·8	89	78·1
No information	1	0·9	—	—
Total	114	100·0	114	100·0

In general the courts were responsive to the suggestion or indication that a medical remand would be useful. Only for four (3·5 per cent) controls would the officer have definitely chosen to have a report.

There were a further 21 (18 per cent) control cases in which the officer thought that it would 'probably be useful' to have a psychiatric report. It will be remembered that doctors were not asked whether a probation officer's report *would* be useful. It seemed unnecessary since no consultant psychiatrist could surely suggest that a report would not be useful. They were asked if the report *had* been useful. It will be remembered that in 9 per cent of cases it had not been of use to them—a somewhat surprising comment when one considers that, at the lowest level of information, it is only the probation officer who can give them reliable information about the previous convictions or whether the offender was convicted. They may have meant that in these cases the report had not contained information which they had not satisfactorily found out for themselves from the offender or his relatives. They would not, however, know whether this was in fact true. In 23 per cent of male cases doctors said they had not seen a report.

The probation officers were not asked whether the medical report *had* been useful. In many cases they would in any case have filled in the questionnaire before receiving the report.

The view, however, that they would have liked a psychiatric report in no less than one in five of control cases raises important issues. If the controls are typical of the general offender population, many hundreds of additional cases would have to be seen, something beyond the capacity of the psychiatric profession. This points to the importance of the selection of cases. These cases do not necessarily require psychiatric treatment. More often the officer may write that he would be reassured if a doctor took the same view as himself about the proposed plan of social treatment and confirmed that he had not overlooked some medical factor. It also points to the need, in drafting a medical report, to write 'past the court' and mention aspects of causation or need which a probation officer may find useful in management.

CHAPTER IX

MEDICAL DEFENCE REPORTS TO MAGISTRATES' COURTS

ALTHOUGH this study was primarily concerned with formal requests by magistrates for a medical report, it seemed useful to consider other sources of medical evidence which might influence the court. All the consultants were asked, therefore, also to fill in a questionnaire for any case on which they were asked to report for defence purposes, and the prison medical officers similarly about any voluntary or unsolicited reports submitted.

Medical information may reach the courts in many different ways. The commonest is probably a letter to the court from the patient's general practitioner. In a previous study of shoplifting we found several letters in which a doctor said, for example, that he was surprised to hear that his patient whom he knew well had been arrested; that she had been under his treatment for depression for several months, and that he felt that such out of character behaviour might well have been affected by this. This may be enough to lead the court to impose a small fine or even give a conditional discharge without much ado. Other letters left the impression by their curtness that the doctor did not really think that a very minor complaint had much to do with the case.

Much sometimes depends upon whether the offender is represented, and intends or is advised to plead guilty. The purpose of a report is not always to establish mental illness or need for treatment in any formal sense. It may be useful in conveying to the court, provided the prosecution agrees, some important aspect of the case which would be unnecessarily painful to a relative if given in open court (e.g. marital infidelity or incest by a parent).

The establishment of the National Health Service, with its corps of consultant psychiatrists, has meant that though reasonable variations of opinion are still preserved, few are likely to believe that in criminal cases the consultant psychiatrist's opinion will vary very widely according to whether the prosecution or the defence call him. If he does over-identify with the defence this is often apparent from his report, and the court may order a remand for another opinion.

We had no means of checking whether consultants remembered to report all their defence examinations to us. In all, 34 psychiatric reports for the defence were presented to magistrates' courts (probably much fewer than in the high courts), about equally divided between males and females, but for men the ratio of reports to formal remands was 18:287 (one in sixteen), for women it was 16:56 (two to seven). This was not because of any greater tendency for women to receive a defence report as well as a formal report. Defence reports tended to be sought for the older offender. Type of offence differed greatly between the sexes. All but one man had committed an indictable offence. Sexual offences (over a quarter of the cases) predominated even more than among the formal remands.

Offences of the females had a much narrower range. Fourteen of the sixteen were indictable (twelve shoplifting and two theft), the remaining two non-indictable offences were unusual—sending offensive telephone messages and 'wasting' police time. In two cases of shoplifting and one of theft, the court also requested a formal medical report.

There was no information about the resulting sentence for five of the eighteen men. There was no Section 60 Hospital Order (compared with 5 per cent of male and 11 per cent of female formal remands); two men out of fifteen received a Section 4 Treatment on Probation Order (if one subtracts the three cases where the court also asked for a formal report). Among the females six out of thirteen received a Section 4 Probation Order (excluding three where the court also asked for a formal report) which is three times the proportion of psychiatric probation orders among the formal remands. At least three of these women had been in contact with a psychiatric hospital in the last year.

Whereas among women formally remanded on bail only 10 per cent were offered treatment on probation (similar to the 11 per cent offered treatment when remanded in custody), 20 per cent of the men remanded for a report on bail received treatment on probation orders as opposed to only 6·5 per cent of those remanded in custody. The recommendation, whether made on formal remand on bail or as the result of a defence report, was made by a hospital consultant and not by a prison medical officer. If the question is whether out-patient treatment, though not essential, would probably be an advantage, the prison medical officer may be reluctant to ask a consultant to come some distance to see the offender and possibly not agree with the need for treatment. If the consultant sees the offender in his clinic he can make his decision at once.

Five males and five females (out of the total 34 defence reports) had been in touch with a psychiatric hospital in the last year, and three more in the last five years. Five of the eight who had medical disposals were in one or other category. In all but two cases the psychiatrists thought the solicitor's referral of the case was reasonable. Two were regarded as sullen or hostile on interview; a much higher proportion were considered anxious and they naturally tended to be very willing to discuss their problems.

The sexes differed greatly in the rating of reliability for out-patient treatment. Only two of the men (11 per cent) were rated as 'very reliable'—a lower proportion than in the large group of formal remands. Half the women were rated as 'very reliable', a dramatic difference from the low proportion among the formal remands. There was no relationship between reliability and a medical sentence, only one 'very reliable' person being given probation with a condition of treatment.

The symptomatic assessment scale, as used before, revealed a very disturbed group. Psychosis was present in 20 per cent of the men—even mild symptoms are, of course, of serious importance; a quarter of the men and 44 per cent of the women had severe or moderate anxiety states. Altogether about half of the defence cases had a fairly serious psychotic or neurotic state. Basic personality ratings showed a similar pattern—four men and five women with a severe rating, nine men and three women with a moderate rating. This again is in contrast to the medical remand group. Intelligence deficiency was usually absent—only two men were moderately dull.

The distribution of alcohol and drug problems was similar to the proportion in court remands—a quarter of both men and women were repeated drinkers or chronic alcoholics. None of these men had a probation order with treatment, three of the women did. Similarly a quarter of both sexes had drug problems, but no man had treatment on a probation order, whereas three of the four women did. No men, and four of the six women with psychiatric probation orders had drink or drug problems.

During the eight-month period two voluntary and unsolicited reports were submitted by prison medical officers.

DEFENCE REPORTS BY THE WESSEX PSYCHIATRISTS

Seventeen psychiatrists wrote at least one defence report during the eight months, and one particular consultant provided no less than ten of the 34 reports. As Chairman of the Regional Board Psychiatric Consultative Group, he was particularly helpful to the present study. This was the late Dr. Foote, whose recent sudden death has been such a loss for forensic psychiatry in the region. He not only saw many defence cases but frequently visited the prisons and admitted many sick offenders to his wards, some of which, he maintained, were staffed by experienced nurses who could manage very difficult patients; he was frequently called also for an independent opinion in prosecution cases. It is characteristic that this impartial and professional attitude to offenders, whether for prosecution or defence, and willingness to offer treatment, should command great respect in the courts and the legal profession.

No other consultant saw more than four cases. There was no apparent relationship between the number of medical remands by the courts and the recorded number of defence reports seen by particular hospital groups. The hospital group which dealt with the largest number of formal medical remands provided a quarter of the defence reports, but the hospital group which dealt with the *second* largest number of court requests (35 per cent of all bailed medical requests) seemed to provide no defence reports at all. The group of hospitals at which Dr. Foote worked, whether or not influenced by him, dealt with 44 per cent of all defence reports.

A defence report was only submitted at 12 courts, no report at 26. The highest number at any court was seven (two for males and five for females). The figure for females is interesting in that during the period there was only one formal request by this court for a report on a female. The three busiest courts in the region for formal reports (contributing 48 per cent of the formal courts requests for medical reports) only contributed 29 per cent of the defence reports.

With such small numbers and the lack of more detailed information one can only speculate about the cause of differences in distribution of formal and defence reports. Small events can influence results of this kind. For example, a large proportion of reports on females was related to shoplifters; a short time before the study a conference of magistrates, probation officers and psychiatrists, was held in one part of the area to discuss the increasing problems of shoplifting. In this particular court there were many subsequent formal requests for a report (perhaps making defence reports unnecessary) while in another there were several defence reports.

One factor which came to light when we visited the consultants at their hospitals was geographical. To remand a woman to Holloway prison in London from the Isle of Wight, involves a long boat and train journey for the offender and, later, the probation officer. There was some indication that defence reports were frequently prepared outside the principal conurbations, perhaps because of the inconvenience of making an appointment at an infrequently held clinic many miles away; a feature which must also affect the capacity to attend for out-patient treatment. In the conurbations with convenient local clinics, the courts are more likely to order formal reports, and there seemed a welcome tendency for the defence to accept the result.

Social class was a factor not easy to assess. In social classes IV and V the response to prosecution is likely to be an expression of guilt and a hope that a few words of mitigation in court might temper the blow. In social classes I to III there is the knowledge to consult a solicitor and to follow his advice and the likelihood of financial support without legal aid. The social stigma of a conviction for dishonesty, e.g. shoplifting, is serious and receives much more publicity, especially in settled cohesive societies outside the anonymous conurbations.

In other respects there are, of course, complex relationships between probation officer, magistrates, solicitors, and psychiatrists—the probation officer who adjusts to the demands of his magistrates in deciding what is or is not possible, the magistrates whose scepticism about psychiatry is mirrored in the local area by the attitudes of offenders themselves and society around them, the solicitor who knows how to approach the local magistrates.

PART III: HIGH COURT STUDY

CHAPTER X

MEDICAL REMANDS BY HIGH COURTS

AFTER completion of the survey of magistrates' courts a supplementary inquiry into remands for medical reports by the high courts was undertaken. To make it as comparable as possible with the magistrates' court study, the information was limited to 1969,[1] to those high courts which received cases from the 18 Inner London magistrates' courts and the 38 magistrates' courts within the Wessex Regional Hospital Board area.

This supplementary study proved to involve complex problems not readily soluble with the means at our disposal. Complete information is probably unobtainable except from the transcript of every trial. Medical evidence reaches the courts from the prosecution or the defence, or at the request of the judge. *The only information available to us concerned requests for medical reports by the judge himself in the court proceedings,*[2] *which may have covered only a small part of the total medical information.* However, although magistrates deal completely with 98 per cent of offenders, the remaining 2 per cent include many serious offenders, who attract most publicity, and the decisions reached as well as the results in appeal cases, have a considerable influence on the operation of the lower courts. Even without full information, the differences in the behaviour of the high courts in the two areas raised interesting questions. Information from London refers to the Inner London Quarter Sessions and the Central Criminal Court; for Wessex, 12 courts of Quarter Sessions, and three County Assizes. In 1969 there were still separate courts of Assize and Quarter Sessions, before the full scale introduction of Crown Courts under the Courts Act of 1971. But as Borrie (1971) says 'no one should imagine that a revolution has occurred in our judicial system just because such deep established institutions as Assizes and Quarter Sessions have been abolished'.

Two classes of offender reach the higher courts. A. Those *committed for trial* at the high court, either because the magistrates have no power to try the offence, or because the offenders elect to be tried by a jury. B. Those *convicted* by the magistrates' court and *committed for sentence* by the high

---

[1] Data was also collected for 1970 and where appropriate we shall consider 1969 and 1970 cases together.

[2] Even the collection of this data was laborious—for London and Wessex Assizes data were available in the court registers, and even here individual court papers had sometimes to be referred to. For Quarter Sessions in Wessex post-trial calendars had to be consulted. For the three London high courts there were pre-trial calendars of court proceedings located at Brixton prison!

court. These include (i) those convicted by the magistrates, but whose 'powers of punishment are not sufficient bearing in mind the offender's character and previous history' (Section 29 Magistrates' Courts Act): (ii) those aged 15 to 21 considered suitable for Borstal training (Section 28 Magistrates' Courts Act): (iii) some who have committed repeated non-indictable offences, committed for sentence as 'incorrigible rogues' under the Vagrancy Act: (iv) those for whom the magistrates have made a Section 60 (Mental Health Act 1959) 'Hospital Order' but consider that an order 'restricting discharge' (Section 65) should be made: (v) those considered 'unfit to plead'; if the offence is serious it must be sent to the high court.

We have to consider those committed for trial separately from the committals for sentence. The great majority were *committals for trial*—in 1972 roughly 51,921 out of a total of 64,551 cases (80 per cent), whereas 4,016 were committed for sentence to Borstal (Section 28), 8,566 for longer sentences than magistrates could impose (Section 29); 20 for Section 65 of the Mental Health Act, 1959, and 28 under the Vagrancy Act. On committal for sentence the magistrates may order a psychiatric report. Defence counsel may consider that full and impressive medical evidence can be presented effectively only if the offender reserves his defence and elects to go for trial. For both these groups—those committed for trial and those committed for sentence—we shall consider the number of medical remands by the judge, the sort of offender remanded, whether custody or bail was used, and the outcome or sentence.

A. Those Committed for Trial

In 1969, 136 persons tried before the Inner London Sessions and the Central Criminal Court were remanded by the judge for a medical report, and 34 by the high courts of Wessex area. In relation to total turnover of the courts concerned, this is 3·08 per cent for London (2·99 per cent for men and 4·27 per cent for women), and 2·26 per cent for Wessex (2·19 per cent men and 2·33 per cent women). However, in London, cases may be remanded to courts other than Inner London Sessions and the Central Criminal Court and an attempt to allow for this[1] suggests that the true London figure may be 4·1 per cent, an excess over Wessex similar to that found in the magistrates' courts. The judges in both areas remanded fewer for medical reports than did the magistrates but these remands were often supplementary to medical evidence already before the court, or because not enough information had been provided.

Ages in Wessex and Inner London were similar. The highest proportion in Inner London was 6·3 per cent for females 17 to 20; in Wessex the highest was 4·3 per cent of females of 30 or over. Of the male offenders, only those aged

---

[1] Consideration of the Supplementary Statistics of criminal proceedings suggest that about one in six cases committed for trial in London are referred to courts other than the two considered, mainly because of over-crowding.

30 or over in London ever approached the figure of 4 per cent for medical remands, the rest were around 2 per cent.

The figures for *indictable offence categories* reflect the magistrates' courts' study, but, as with age, within a narrower range. Among males sexual offenders accounted for the highest proportion of medical remands (7·1 per cent in London, 5·3 per cent in Wessex). In Wessex, an exceptional proportion of those committing 'other' offences (all *arson*)—23 per cent or eight out of 35 cases—were medically remanded. The females who committed the unusual offences of 'violence to the person' were those most often remanded for a medical report (7·1 per cent of London and 5·6 per cent of Wessex cases) but there were only four cases in the two areas together.

As we said, some offenders who have only committed *non-indictable* offences may come for trial at higher courts. In this series, offences leading to medical remands included malicious damage, importuning by a male, living on immoral earnings, offences against the dangerous drugs act, driving a vehicle when disqualified, and impersonating a police officer. There were 18 (15 male, 3 female) in London, but none in Wessex. It is thus a particularly London phenomenon.[1]

This echoed the magistrates' courts' study, in which 'Inner London magistrates provided thirteen times as many male and nearly fifty times as many female "nuisance" offenders for the doctors to consider as is the case in the Wessex area' (Soothill and Pope, 1974).

An examination of whether the medical remands by the high courts were made on bail or custody—the starting point of this survey—gave surprising results. The samples considered were those in 1969 and 1970 in London and Wessex.

For the 289 cases from Inner London courts the use of bail by the high courts was similar to that of the magistrates' courts: 89 per cent were medically remanded in custody (91 per cent of the males and 76 per cent of the 29 females); and 11 per cent were bailed (9 per cent of males: 24 per cent of females). In Wessex, of the 67 male medical remands only two were remanded on bail; of the five women none was bailed for a medical report.

When the information about types of remand and committal and types of medical remand by the high courts is combined, the trend becomes clearer, and as it is similar in Wessex and London we shall consider together the total of 348 cases about which there is complete information.

There were four patterns of remand. (A) Custody for both committal for trial and medical remand by the high court—59 per cent. (B) Bail on committal but custody for the medical remand—33 per cent. (C) Bail both for

---

[1] It is unfortunately impossible to find out from the Criminal Statistics the relative frequency with which non-indictable offenders are medically examined, for it is stated that 'if a person is prosecuted on the same occasion for both indictable and non-indictable offences, he is recorded once in the indictable offence section of the appropriate table, and is also recorded once in the non-indictable offence section'. (Criminal Statistics of England and Wales, 1969, Cmnd. 4398, p. 18.)

committal and for medical remand—8 per cent. (D) Custody on committal but bail for the medical remand—only one per cent.

The sentences after these medical remands by the judges (see TABLE 3 8), show that of those in custody throughout no less than 31 per cent did not subsequently receive a custodial sentence (possibly 38 per cent if we assume that Section 4 psychiatric treatment on probation referred to out-patient treatment). It is sometimes argued that because an offender has already

TABLE 38

CUSTODY OR BAIL FOR MEDICAL REMAND BY HIGH COURTS
(LONDON AND WESSEX COMBINED)

Sentences	A. *Custody Group* (*Custody for both committal and medical remand*)		B. *Discrepant Group* (*Bailed at committal: custody for medical remand*)		C. *Bail Group* (*Bail for both committal and medical remand*)	
	No.	%	*No.*	%	*No.*	%
Non-custodial	64	31·2	63	55·2	12	46·2
Custodial	101	49·3	42	36·9	11	42·3
Medical Sentences						
S4	13	6·3	7	6·1	1	3·8
S60	19	9·3	2	1·8	0	0·0
No information	8	3·9	0	0·0	2	7·7
Total	205	100·0	114	100·0	26	100·0

We have disregarded the three persons in Group D who were actually committed in custody but who were subsequently remanded on bail for a medical report.

spent between two and four months in custody the court can take a more lenient view of the sentence, especially if reports are favourable. Even so, however, the proportion receiving non-custodial sentences was exceptionally high and raises the question of the need for custody. Of the remainder, 23 per cent received a prison sentence of up to two years, 22 per cent received one of two years or more and 5 per cent went to young offender institutions. Of those in custody since committal, often for two to four months, the custodial medical remand was completed in over a third (35 per cent) in 15 days but 21 per cent were in custody for a further 30 days or more.

The second, or 'discrepant', group B, committed for trial on bail but remanded for a medical report in custody, raises a different issue. If they were committed on bail why were they remanded in custody for a medical report? There are various possible explanations. If a medical report was submitted by the defence but the judge did not know the writer and the report was strongly 'excusatory', he might have wished to know whether a prison medical officer agreed. New issues might have arisen, e.g. a psychiatric probation order might have been suggested by the defence but the judge might have wondered whether a Section 60 would be preferable. A man might have stated his intention to plead not guilty, in such cases the probation service, especially in London, frequently does not prepare a social inquiry report. Very experienced offenders might have refused to be interviewed.

Many of the remands might have been preceeded by a finding of guilt at the trial. Experience of one of us on the Parole Board, where these stages are fully recorded, suggests that courts and prisoners take a different view of bail after conviction. Experienced or professional offenders can often be bailed before trial with almost complete safety, since they are often 'risk taking' individuals who easily persuade themselves that their defence will be successful. To an astonishing extent they are careful while on bail to avoid further detectable criminal behaviour.[1] Once convicted, however, they may think that their record is bound to attract a prison sentence and the temptation to abscond, therefore, greatly increases; moreover, the presumption of innocence has disappeared and the judge feels justified in making a remand in custody.

The 'discrepant' group were possibly less serious offenders; no less than 55 per cent received a non-custodial sentence (22 per cent suspended sentences and 25 per cent probation order), and prison sentences were less severe (12 per cent receiving two years or more compared with 22 per cent of those receiving continuous custody after arrest). Hospital orders were much less frequently the outcome of the report. The total medical effect of this later remand in custody for the 114 people was negligible, unless the object was merely to exclude psychiatric abnormality. No less than 17 per cent, having been on bail before, spent a month or more in prison for the report; 49 per cent were remanded only for up to 15 days.

Group C, on bail throughout until sentence, received no hospital orders, but a surprisingly large proportion (31 per cent) received a prison sentence; altogether 42 per cent received a custodial sentence of some type (including Borstal or detention centre).

The sentences imposed on the medical remands by high courts were very different in the two areas (as in the magistrates' courts).

The larger proportion of Wessex medical disposals was largely accounted for by the higher proportion of offenders offered treatment on probation (Section 4, Criminal Justice Act, 1948). The women offenders were too few (29 in London and six in Wessex) to be expressed in detailed percentages. In London 16 women were given non-custodial sentences, four women received Section 4 psychiatric probation orders and one hospital order was made.

Previous medical and penal treatment. A recent study of persons who had *repeated* medical remands (i.e. had twice in one year been remanded for a medical report on separate occasions for separate offences (Soothill, 1974)) showed that males seldom received a psychiatric disposal unless they had had previous in-patient psychiatric treatment; but for women there was not the same relationship between psychiatric disposal and previous hospital treatment, no doubt because women offenders tend to show more florid personality

---

[1] The rare exceptions include very unstable and impulsive offenders who carry on committing offences, and a few who possibly feel that they are bound to be 'put away' and decide to obtain a 'nest egg' for their wives to support them while they are away!

disorders with hysterical outbursts or repeated suicidal attempts, and are more readily regarded by psychiatrists as psychiatrically disordered.

Repeated medical remands in males mainly related to alcoholic, unstable, and homeless petty recidivists (i.e. the courts were tacitly asking the doctors for suggestions about medical or social care). Throughout this study there has

TABLE 39

SENTENCES IMPOSED ON MALES MEDICALLY
REMANDED BY HIGH COURTS DURING OR AFTER
TRIAL (LONDON AND WESSEX 1969 AND 1970)

Sentences	Males Inner London %	Wessex %
Non-custodial	38·6	40·3
Custodial	48·0	34·3
Medical—S4 (CJA 1948)	2·6 } 8·9	13·4 } 23·9
S60 (MHA 1959)	6·3	10·5
No information	4·5	1·5
Total	100·0	100·0
	(269)	(67)

been the constant doubt as to whether the offenders coming before the Inner London and Wessex courts were 'quite different' and whether this was the main factor in the different treatment. Our view is that although there *are* differences in the offenders they cannot entirely account for the differences in treatment by the courts, due in part to differences in treatment in the probation service, the loads borne by the courts, and the available medical facilities. It is useful, therefore, to compare the medical remands by the high courts in the two areas in the light of previous medical disposals by the courts of all types, and the nature and frequency of previous offences.

The Inner London sample was restricted to previous convictions and disposal data for 1969; these were traced for 131 of the 150 persons. For Wessex, since further data were available and the total numbers much smaller, we combined the figures for 1969 and 1970, information being available for 63 of the 73 persons. Females were so few that they were excluded.

The number of *previous* convictions of the London and Wessex samples of males medically remanded by the high court was remarkably similar, e.g. 27 per cent in London and 25 per cent in Wessex were first offenders. Multi-recidivism was slightly higher in the London sample, e.g. 5–9 previous convictions, 25 per cent in London *against* 20 per cent in Wessex; 10 or more previous convictions, 19 per cent in London, 15 per cent in Wessex. Altogether, 44 per cent in London and 36 per cent in Wessex had five or more previous convictions.

Previous type of offence also showed remarkably little difference, what there was mainly related to the larger number with previous convictions, particularly for property offences, in the London sample. Inner London had more previous drug offences, 8·8 per cent against 3·4 per cent in Wessex, and Wessex more previous sexual offences, 15·3 per cent against 6·2 per cent in London.

Previous medical disposals by a court were also fairly similar; 7·1 per cent of London and 3·4 per cent of Wessex had had a previous Section 60 hospital order and 5·3 per cent in London and 8·5 per cent in Wessex a previous Section 4 psychiatric probation order. London cases had had rather more previous custodial sentences, especially approved school training as juveniles (15 per cent compared with 8·5 per cent in Wessex) and 44·2 per cent previous prison sentences compared with 37·3 per cent in Wessex.

Lastly, since the higher courts' study was comparable with the magistrates' courts' study, it was possible to find out how many of those committed for trial by the high courts had a *previous medical remand at the magistrates' courts*. In London 99 persons (84 men and 15 women) were committed for trial in 1969 after the magistrates had obtained a medical report, but only four in Wessex. In the London high courts no medical remands or medical disposals were ordered in 75 (89·3 per cent) cases. In three cases the high court ordered another medical remand and made a medical disposal, in four cases there was a further high court medical remand but no medical disposal, in two cases there was no further medical remand but a medical disposal was made. When the high court knows that there has been a medical report to the magistrates this clearly influences their freedom of action in that a medical disposal or doubt has been ruled out or removed. Some of the complications are revealed in the following case:

A man of 37 accused of burglary was ordered to receive a medical report at the time of committal, with regard to fitness to plead. At the Inner London sessions a post-trial remand for a further independent medical report was ordered. He was remanded again with a view to a Section 60; further remanded to find a place in a hospital, remanded again until a time when a doctor could attend, and remanded again before being sentenced to a Section 60 hospital order with Section 65 restriction order without limit of time.

B. Committals for Sentence to a Higher Court

This group of cases had been tried and convicted by the magistrates, but committed for sentence to the high court. They were offenders for whom the magistrates found their powers of sentence too limited. In this situation the decisions of the two courts were more nearly balanced, the magistrates receiving a great deal more information. The Magistrates' Courts Act, 1952 (Section 29) requires them to commit for sentence only 'on obtaining information about his character and antecedents' and when considering a Borstal sentence 'they must consider . . . the offender's physical and mental condition and his suitability for his training' (Section 28, Magistrates' Courts Act, 1952). Magistrates cannot impose a Section 65 restriction order in addition to a Section 60 hospital order, nor deal with unfitness to plead.

Among indictable offenders the court registers showed that 71 persons were remanded by the Central Criminal Court in the Inner London sessions for a medical report before sentence and 12 persons in Wessex. For reasons discussed earlier the proportion in relation to the total court turnover in London might be an underestimate but among males this probably represented 4·1 per cent of indictable offenders. It is remarkable that for females the figure was 18·8 per cent (or 12 out of 64) in the total court turnover. In Wessex there were no medical remands of females, and 12 among 346 cases or 3·5 per cent for males, lower, as always, than in the London courts.

The magistrates, as we saw, concentrated their medical inquiries mainly on the younger age groups and those sent to Borstal sentence had usually been fully investigated. Those medically remanded by the high courts were the complete opposite. Among men, 1·9 per cent in the 17–20 age group, 4·7 per cent in the 21–29 group and 6·3 per cent in the 30 and over group were remanded; the Wessex cases were very similar. Among London women, however, 6·3 per cent were 17–20, 21·4 per cent 21–29, and no less than 38·9 per cent were aged 30 or over (7 out of 18 cases). In type of crime there was little variation in Wessex with the three or four per cent of men in each offence category being medically remanded and the same applied to men in London. For every sort of offence for males no category exceeded 7 per cent in the proportion of medical remands except for sixteen male sex offenders in London of whom 25 per cent were remanded. Among the London women 20·9 per cent of the 43 convicted of theft, shoplifting or handling were remanded, and 14·3 per cent of the 14 convicted of fraud or forgery. The judges, with their eyes upon general deterrence, had little opportunity to be flexible with so many male offenders, and so might be all the more willing to be lenient with women offenders, who offer little threat to public safety and are less likely to know or be influenced by what happens to other women offenders.

In London only eleven persons (9 men and 2 women) convicted of non-indictable offences were remanded; two (1 man and 1 women) in Wessex. None received a medical disposal.

So far as *custody and bail* were concerned, since the magistrates had considered that they had insufficient powers of punishment, it was to be expected that nearly all offenders would be remanded in custody. In both areas those committed for sentence in two years (1969 and 1970) were considered. In fact, custody was not always used. In London about one in twenty males were committed for sentence on bail and one in five women. In Wessex about one in eight males were bailed but apparently no women.

Similarly when the high courts remanded for a medical report it was almost invariably in custody; there was only one remand on bail, a Wessex case. The time spent on these further remands, which was, of course, additional to the time spent awaiting appearance before the high court, was more often much shorter than in trial cases—in only 10·7 per cent the sentence was delayed for a further 30 days or more, and in a third it was up to 15 days.

In respect of *final sentence* on those medically remanded by the high court, of the total sample in both areas in 1969 and 1970 (181 cases) only nine hospital orders (in at least five of whom a Section 65 restriction order was made) and seven psychiatric probation orders were made. The most remarkable aspect of the sentences, however, considering that the magistrates were presumed not to have sufficient powers of punishment, was that a high proportion received *non-custodial sentences*—in Inner London 29 per cent of men, 63 per cent of women; in Wessex 52 per cent of men, 20 per cent of women. Only 100 (55 per cent) received sentences which were beyond the magistrates' powers. There are several possible explanations—that mitigating circumstances or transitory mental disorders came to light, or accomplices or co-charged offenders on investigation were found to have played a smaller part in the offence. The magistrates undoubtedly committed a few for sentence as a severe warning when they thought that an offender had taken the offence far too lightly and felt over-confident that he would 'only be put on probation'.

Since these are cases for whom the magistrates have power to convict, they could be expected to refer to relatively minor crimes committed by men with a long criminal record or of rapidly repeated offences. This was borne out by the *previous criminal record* in the 76 cases for whom there is information. Nearly a third (30 per cent in London, 32 per cent in Wessex) had ten or more previous convictions. Two-thirds in both areas had five or more previous convictions, whereas this is so in less than half of the 'trial' cases. Although only 9 per cent of Wessex cases had fewer than three previous convictions, this was true of 20 per cent of London men who might have belonged to the group who took the offence far too lightly.

In *type of crime* there were fewer problematical or exceptional cases, such as sexual or drug offences. Two-thirds were theft, handling, etc., with previous records of property offences.

The *previous sentences* included *previous medical disposals* in 13 per cent of London males and 18 per cent of Wessex males; but none received a medical disposal in the current case. Having checked on present mental state, the judges had presumably concluded that further psychiatric treatment, at least outside prison, was no longer appropriate.

Since the higher courts' study was comparable with the magistrates' courts' study it was possible to estimate how many of those committed for sentence with a *previous medical remand at the magistrates' courts* also had a medical remand at the high court level. There was evidence that there had been a medical remand by both the magistrates *and* the high court in 4 per cent of males and 7 per cent of females in London and 4 per cent of males but no females in Wessex. Although 22 people in London and Wessex received two medical inquiries, only two received medical disposals in consequence, and nearly a third of them were given a non-custodial sentence.

Those medically remanded by both the magistrates and the high courts revealed no special characteristics in respect of age, sex or type of offence.

PART IV

CHAPTER XI

SUMMARY AND CONCLUSIONS

THE results of this study have been set out in considerable detail, and it may be convenient to draw together the main results and comment upon them.

The retrospective study, comprising all the medical reports requested in 1969 by 18 Inner London magistrates' courts and the 34 courts within the Wessex Regional Hospital Board Area, consisted of relatively crude data (age, sex, offence, passage through the courts, sentence) and was related to the total turnover of the courts—similar details of all offenders coming before each of these courts. This showed that medical reports were rarely requested. But the proportion of reports for indictable offences (not necessarily serious, for all theft is indictable) and the mass of non-indictable offences—breaches of regulations, motoring offences, and the like, but including some offences regarded generally as significant in relation to the offender's personality and social adjustment—alcohol and drug offences, some sexual offences—differed considerably. Among the smaller number of indictable offences a substantial proportion were remanded for medical reports—nearly one in ten as compared with one in a hundred for non-indictable offences.

Indictable offences were considered separately. The proportion examined medically in Wessex was smaller than in London.

Age was relevant. In London young males (17–21) were more frequently examined medically than in Wessex. The trend was reversed for females. The large differences in London for young adult males was almost certainly due to the number of 'Borstal eligible' youths in the large conurbations, who tended to be sent to the Crown Court for a Borstal report by the governor of the remand centre with a request for a medical report, to give the fullest information on which to select those suitable for a Borstal sentence. Outside the main conurbations the criteria for Borstal were less severe—'eligibles' had fewer previous convictions—perhaps because there are fewer of them. In a previous study (Gibbens, 1963) this conclusion appeared to be unavoidable. Females of this age have to go to Holloway remand centre or Puckle-church (near Bristol) for a report, and thus there is probably a tendency to obtain the maximum information locally before deciding upon such a course. Apart from this excess of youthful remands in London, there were no great age differences.

The nature of the offence made a difference, particularly for male sex offenders and for women who had committed 'odd' offences—burglary, fraud, etc. (possibly in relation to drug offences (e.g. forged prescriptions)). Violence was not prominent perhaps because on a small scale it is often 'understandable', and on a large scale usually involves referral to the Crown Court.

The outcome of the report—*the sentence*—revealed the most significant difference. Wessex courts asked for fewer reports, but made a medical treatment disposal in a higher proportion. In Inner London a Section 60 Hospital Order was made in 4·5 per cent of cases but in 6·7 per cent in Wessex. Even more striking, though only 2·7 per cent received a probation order with psychiatric treatment in London, 15·1 per cent received one in Wessex. There may be many reasons for this apparently more effective and economical selection of cases in Wessex but, two were almost certainly crucial. (1) The probation service in Wessex, but not in London, made a pre-trial report on nearly all cases, and elicited a history of previous breakdown or recent psychiatric treatment in a high proportion of selected cases. (2) A higher proportion of offenders were remanded on *bail* in Wessex for reports by N.H.S. consultants who were more likely to pick out those they were willing to treat, without previous selection by a prison medical officer. Psychiatric treatment was more likely to be ordered for sex offenders in both areas; and, among women for offences against property with violence, or fraud and forgery (possibly connected with drug taking). Psychiatric cases showed about the same age distribution in the two areas, being rather commoner among men over 30 and younger women of 17–20.

Non-indictable offences showed marked differences of another sort. Very few minor offenders received a medical examination in London and even fewer in Wessex, mainly in the 17–20 age group. But several offences implied considerable personal maladjustment—indecent exposure, importuning by males, prostitution, begging, sleeping out, and some drug offences, and a higher proportion of these were medically examined in Inner London. Few of these offenders received a medical disposal although other social support might have resulted, but again proportionately more were ordered in Wessex, especially for women.

The non-indictable offences, however, raised the question of whether the offender population in London differed fundamentally from that in Wessex. London probably attracts the vagrant psychotic, and young people whose behaviour has made them unpopular with their families and too well-known in local society, and generates its own problems in deteriorated areas. The London courts dealt with 30,000 drunken offences compared with 2,000 in Wessex and the 0·5 per cent medically remanded in London amounted to 148 for this offence alone, that is, nearly as many as the 180 medical reports on *all* 55,000 non-indictable offenders reported on in Wessex.

The Court Process. In Inner London just over half of those subsequently medically remanded received no bail (that is, were kept in custody from before midnight on the day before court appearance); bail probably did not arise with one quarter who appeared in court the same day (that is, from after midnight). In Wessex, where some courts sit only once or twice a week, police bail had more importance.

The 289 (7 per cent) pre-trial medical remands were a phenomenon peculiar to London. Wessex used this method in less than one per cent. The London courts differed widely in their use of it, which left them free, if suitable, to make a medical committal without recording a conviction. Most of those remanded in London related to violent assaultive or disorderly behaviour; about half were non-indictable, and the outcome showed that as a group these offenders were especially disordered.

The remand in custody to obtain a medical report—the original focus of our study—was much more used in London than in Wessex. In Wessex, moreover, the recognizances and sureties demanded were smaller in amount, and overall a higher proportion were remanded on bail—*whatever the category of offence.* Yet again, in London more offenders had a medical remand in custody in spite of a period of bail earlier in the court process. *A quarter of the custodial medical remands had had a previous period of bail (police or court).* Differences in the type of offender, even though fairly considerable, did not account for the large difference in the use of medical remands on bail in the areas. The London courts differed from one another considerably in the use of bail—one ordering custody throughout the court process for 80 per cent, another 54 per cent on bail at some stage. It was probably not fortuitous that the busiest courts had the highest rates of custodial remands. Where speed is important the custodial remand is dangerously easy to administer.

There may be three major reasons for this apparently excessive use in London of the remand in custody for reports, unconnected with the defendant's likely attendance in court. Difficulties in finding an N.H.S. clinic for a report upon the offender on bail does arise, but it is not a major reason.[1] 'Bail clinics', which are tantamount to out-patient facilities, exist for women at Holloway prison and for men at Brixton prison. They were at first restricted to the use of only a few courts lest they be overwhelmed with requests, but this did not occur and when they were extended to a wider range of courts the demand has been very slow to develop; in the first half of 1975 there were only 45 requests at Brixton.

The courts may prefer a report from the prison medical service (associating this with custody though it could be obtained on bail). The service has great experience with offenders, knows the resources of the prison service, is officially appointed as medical adviser to the courts, and above all, is guaranteed to report in the required three weeks. This undoubtedly has some weight. An eminent and experienced magistrate, chairman of his bench just outside London, assured one of us that his senior probation officer had told

---

[1] In 1974 the *Report of the Work of the Prison Department* (para. 90) when discussing failure of courts to use the out-patient facilities observed 'comments from the London courts indicated that in general they found the facilities at local hospitals were adequate'.

the court that 'if a medical report is required, it must be in custody'. This was not, of course, true; but an overworked probation service may have preferred this solution. Many magistrates may believe that 'daily observation' in custody will lead to a more thorough and reliable assessment. This would be true of psychotic or more grossly disordered offenders, but the great majority of less obviously disturbed offenders are kept in ordinary cells until called for an interview for an hour or less, similar to that provided by a Health Service consultant. There were hints that the attitude of offenders at interview might differ according to whether they were seen in custody or on bail.

The courts might prefer a remand in custody not only because it may produce useful information but also because it may act as a warning to the offender of what faces him if he persists in his present behaviour. Magistrates admit that the fact that an offender has already spent three weeks in custody—perhaps much longer—enables them to reduce the final sentence to a non-custodial one. In a sense the offender has already been in prison—three weeks in custody under conditions only slightly different from those provided for sentenced prisoners. But custody is a two-edged weapon. For the inexperienced it may act as a warning, sometimes a devastating one; but for some repeated offenders who have not had adult custodial experience, custody in prison or a remand centre for the first time may have few terrors, surrounded by friends who regard it lightly, and the fear of imprisonment may lose much of its force. Our more detailed study in Wessex suggested that local doctors found relatively few medical remands to be unnecessary.

It is probably more profitable to consider whether current practice is well adapted to its objective of an appropriate sentence and the provision of psychiatric help for those who need or could respond to it.

Our study of the resulting sentences showed that in London much less use was made of hospital or probation orders with treatment than in Wessex and that the proportion of hospital orders was greater than that of psychiatric probation orders. It is extremely unlikely that in any fairly wide range of referrals those severely ill should out-number those who have lesser disabilities suitable for treatment on probation. The Wessex figures conformed more closely to reality.

Apart from medical disposals there are some differences in sentencing practice in the two areas. Custodial sentences were a little lower in Wessex, as were the proportions of those bound over or given a conditional discharge, but probation orders were higher. There was no clear relationship between remand in custody and a custodial sentence.

The psychiatrically more efficient use of available resources in Wessex seems clearly due to the use of bail and referrals to consultants in the Health Service. Conversely, so long as the prison medical service and the National Health psychiatric service are separate an increase in remands in custody is unlikely to produce any advance in the psychiatric treatment of offenders of all types, especially of the great and increasing number of those not sent to any form of imprisonment. The prison medical officers have a greater experience of serious offenders of all types, especially recidivists, and knowledge of the facilities for psychiatric treatment and support within prisons. This inevitably leads to less experience of the extent to which facilities for the treatment of abnormal offenders can be successfully applied in the community. They have an important function in advising on the existence of psychosis or other severe disorder, the neglect of which by the court would lead to a miscarriage of justice. But they also have a duty to see that justice is administered by the court and not by doctors, and that extreme or eccentric psychiatric views are not allowed to exert undue influence on the courts.

This dilemma has been partly reduced by the establishment of joint appointments between the N.H.S. and the prison service, in which a consultant has a part-time appointment in the prison service and also an in-patient and out-patient service in the Health Service. In this way he has a contemporary experience of both types of work and a specialized knowledge of the characteristics and treatment of offenders in both fields. Whether the offender is remanded in custody or on bail the same psychiatrist may be reporting to the court.

The Prospective Study (PART II) was carried out in Wessex in the eight months from September 1970–April 1971, with the participation of the probation officers and the consultant psychiatrists in the region.

We expected to find little change from the previous year in the pattern of action by the courts and doctors but medical remands had increased, as had remands on bail for reports. The probable explanation is that the 1967 Criminal Justice Act was beginning to have an effect. Though this limits the use of remand in custody to certain restricted classes of offender, clerks and courts might have come to recognize that remand on bail was practicable, and that custody could not be justified.

An interesting aspect of this part of the study related to the *involvement of N.H.S. psychiatric consultants in forensic work*. The bail cases referred for a medical report were examined by 39 consultants, of which seven worked outside the Wessex Hospital Board area, and of the 41 consultants or acting consultants in the area all but nine wrote a remand report during the period. Moreover, all but two of these nine had experience of forensic work during the eight-month period either as visiting psychotherapist to a prison or a specialist in alcoholism or drug addiction etc. So virtually all the consultants were involved in forensic work, though unequally. For example, four consultants between them saw 52 (38 per cent) of the remands on bail. This concentration of a few consultants on forensic work was due not only to interest and willingness to collaborate, but also to having mainly male beds in their hospitals, and wards suitable for, and nursing staff experienced in, forensic cases. In hospitals, bail requests tended to be allocated to consultants known to be interested in such patients.

Only in 5 per cent of the bail cases did the time taken to supply a report exceed four weeks. The main reason for delay was the time needed to examine the patient during a busy regular out-patient afternoon. Thus the tendency was to offer an appointment at another time. However, nowadays many consultants maintain out-patient clinics in large towns for the convenience of follow-up treatment of discharged cases and convenient centres are increasingly available, and nearly all the consultants said they would have been willing to see more cases. The examination averaged an hour but for custody cases the consultant's travelling time had to be added. This may be a reason why so few Section 4 psychiatric probation orders are made by prison doctors. Thus, the custody cases were seen mainly by prison medical officers, in Winchester prison and remand centre, Dorchester prison and a few in Holloway prison, Exeter and Pucklechurch remand centres. As with the consultants a few doctors dealt with the majority; 86 per cent of the reports were prepared by only four of the 15 prison doctors. There were, of course, many cases (e.g. hospital orders) in which several doctors are involved at different stages or in consultation and collaboration.

Physical and Mental Health. Physical ill health or disability was considered by the doctors to be a moderate or serious problem in 15 per cent of males and 32 per cent of females. About half of the offenders had a history of previous psychiatric treatment. The high proportion with evidence of previous general or mental hospital attendance among the remands was almost certainly affected by the practice in Wessex for the majority of offenders to receive a pre-trial probation interview which would tend to elicit such evidence. In London few probation reports can be prepared, and the magistrates often have to depend upon the accused's demeanour or statements. The psychiatrists' views of the *present mental state* of those remanded are difficult to summarize. Only 11 per cent of men and 5 per cent of women had any severe rating on symptoms and 70 per cent of men and 66 per cent of women were assessed as having mild or no symptoms. 'Other neurotic symptoms' was a category frequently used by prison medical officers, perhaps because the use of 'anxiety state' might be misunderstood by lay magistrates as having no pathological significance. Personality disorders were more frequently severe. Mental retardation, which could coexist with other categories, was severe in only 2 per cent of men and women. When mental disorders and personality disorders were combined, 30 per cent of the men and 28 per cent of the women were considered to have minor or no problems in either field of mental health.

About a quarter of both sexes were regarded as chronic alcoholics or repeated drinkers (all but three (men) were over 30), generally in association with mental or personality disorders. The women had a higher incidence of drinking problems, and more were regarded as having a personality disorder in addition.

Drug abuse tended to involve the younger age group, and more women than men, and nearly all were regarded as having personality disorders of some degree.

Only eight offenders showed no abnormality.

The relationship between disorders of both kinds and the *sentence of the court* was complex. Severely disordered offenders tended to receive a medical disposal or non-custodial sentence, disposals being to some extent related to previous criminal record. The medical remands tended to be older and to have many more previous convictions than the general run of offenders before the courts (especially in the case of women) and their previous record tended to relate to previous adult convictions rather than juvenile ones, suggesting a late breakdown in social adjustment, though this comment is made with some reservations as a juvenile record is not always reported if any offender has several adult convictions.

Offences were overwhelmingly against property. The proportion of offences of violence was low in relation to the high rate of alcoholism and was equal for men and women. Sexual offenders tended to be singled out for medical examination; drug offences were infrequent. About 15 per cent of offenders had had either a previous psychiatric probation order or hospital order.

These clinical details demonstrated that the Wessex sample, of which so many were remanded on bail for a medical report, were not composed of relatively problem-free first offenders, but included a high proportion of disordered and recidivist offenders who presented a serious problem to the court. This also emerged from the comparison of a sample of medical remands compared with a control sample of other offenders.

The commonest reasons for a medical remand were (*a*) knowledge or suspicion of previous mental illness, (*b*) the nature of the present offence. Occasionally a medical report seemed to be requested in addition to others 'for good measure'. The request for a report did not seem justified for 12 per cent of men and 7 per cent of women. However, nearly all the requests not thought justified arose from custodial remands and accounted for almost one in five of reports by prison medical officers. Offenders on bail were reported as more sullen, hostile, and anxious, and less friendly, than those seen in custody.

Only seldom were previous records not supplied to the examining doctor but probation reports were lacking in between a quarter and a third of the cases. A large proportion of offenders, particularly those seen in custody, were regarded as unreliable for out-patient treatment.

Recommendations for in-patient treatment were with one exception accepted by the courts. A recommendation for a psychiatric probation order was accepted in 69 per cent of cases; the offender is, of course, entitled to decline such an offer when he appears in court.

It is probable that doctors tended to recommend the sort of treatment with which they were most familiar. All the recommendations for treatment in prison and all but one of those for institutional sentence were made by prison doctors; whereas 71 per cent of the recommendations for supportive environments (hostels, sheltered communities, etc.) were made by consultants. Thus the choice of bail or custody may determine the type of advice.

The Control Sample. Although the selection of medical remands appeared representative on a number of criteria, the controls showed a considerable bias towards youthful offenders (greater than in the total court turnover). The main interest lay in the information about the social background of the medical remands.

The medical remands included many more middle-aged, had more previous convictions, mainly in adult life, as well as prison sentences, but fewer juvenile offences, and had lived for a shorter period in Wessex. A high proportion of men were single and a greater proportion had separated or been divorced especially in the last three years. A higher proportion were of no fixed abode and socially isolated—living alone or sleeping rough, out of contact with near relatives, and unemployed. The controls, though younger, had more contact with a general hospital in the last year for some physical complaint than the medical remands; but previous contact with psychiatric hospitals was almost entirely confined to the medical remands, indicating no doubt that information from the probation service had had much influence on the court.

Our study of the nature of the disorders—social and medical—among the remanded population was thus principally of value in suggesting that the high rate of referral, and on bail, to the consultants in Wessex could not be attributed, at least to any major extent, to the fact that the type of offender was less mobile and disordered than in London. Our conclusion, at least, is that the difference in the two areas is mainly due to the practice of the courts, and in particular to the different work-load of the probation service, rather than to major differences in the type of offender.

Medical Reports for the Defence. Although our concern was with official court requests for reports, it seemed useful to find out the extent to which defence reports were requested in addition to the formal requests. In fact consultants submitted to magistrates' courts relatively few reports for the defence. These referred to a somewhat older age group than the formal remands, and were proportionately four times more for women than for men; two defence reports for every seven formal ones, compared with one for every 16 formal reports on men. About one-third of the 16 reports on females led to psychiatric probation orders.

The prospective study concentrated on Wessex, because of the complications and difficulties of such a London study, but in a supplementary inquiry into remands for medical reports by the *high* courts, we considered both areas—Inner London and Wessex.

The high court situation about medical evidence was complicated and we, therefore, concentrated on those cases in which the high court judge himself remanded for a medical report. These represented an unknown proportion, possibly a minority, of the cases in which medical evidence was produced, and tended to be the residual cases where neither defence nor prison medical service produced sufficient medical information to enable the judge to be confident about the most appropriate sentence, or the judge was not prepared to accept the medical evidence produced by the defence, or a new situation arose (e.g. the accused fell ill). Although we term this a residual category, what did emerge was that the judge often remanded for a medical report, perhaps more than might have been expected had full preparations been made.

The high court study was retrospective and to make it as comparable as possible with the retrospective magistrates' courts' study (PART I) it was restricted to the same areas and time-span.[1] Although at the time of the study, there were still separate courts of Assize and Quarter Sessions, it is unlikely that the Courts Act, 1971, and the full-scale introduction of Crown Courts have much affected the procedures of medical remands.

An important distinction has to be made between two groups appearing before the high courts—those committed for *trial* by the high court and those convicted by the magistrates' court and committed for *sentence* by the high court. But, whatever function the high court is carrying out, it is clear that in recent years clashes in psychiatric evidence are rare. Since the introduction of the National Health Service, controversy has become much more limited in practice. What is often overlooked is that only consultant psychiatrists are in the final analysis likely to carry weight with the court, and these consultants are increasingly likely to have had a generally accepted system of comprehensive training, so that their opinions are likely to show only marginal or minor differences, important though these may be in the individual case.

Committed for Trial to a Higher Court. High Court remands for a medical report in indictable offences were proportionately nearly twice as many in London as in Wessex. The proportions remanded for a medical report within various indictable offence categories paralleled the results of the lower court study though the ranges were narrower. Sexual offences by men, offences against property with violence by women provoked the largest proportion of medical remands.

London high courts were more inclined to remand *on bail* for a medical report than Wessex courts, and there was a sharp reduction in bail cases in Wessex. One third of all the trial cases in the sample were committed *on bail* and then subsequently remanded in custody for a medical report, although the majority of this group then received *non-custodial* sentences.

Formal medical disposals were, however, nearly three times higher in Wessex than in London possibly because of the greater willingness of Wessex psychiatrists to accept and Wessex courts to impose psychiatric probation

[1] In fact, as well as for the year 1969, data was also collected for 1970 and on appropriate occasions we considered 1969 and 1970 cases together.

orders, since apart from the fact that London offenders had longer criminal records, the type of offender did not appear greatly to differ.

Committed for Sentence to a Higher Court. With these cases, as the trial had been held in the lower court, there were, of course, opportunities for a medical report to be obtained before the case reached the high court. Even so, a remarkably high proportion were remanded for a medical report by high courts, London courts as before remanding a higher proportion particularly of older women for a medical report. The small numbers of young males and females probably reflected the fact that they were eligible for a sentence of Borstal training and a medical report would have been requested by the magistrates' court before they were committed for sentence.

The numbers of those whose sentence was a medical disposal were higher in Wessex for both males and females. What was noteworthy was the high proportion given non-custodial (and non-medical) sentences in both areas, for one would have expected sentences beyond the powers of magistrates to impose. Indeed, only half received sentences which needed the imprint of a high court.

There are several possible explanations. Judges note (sometimes publicly) the period already spent in custody. This period might have made it possible to pass a non-custodial sentence. Medical and probation inquiries might have revealed mitigating circumstances, or transitory mental disturbance not requiring further treatment. Judges and some magistrates might have had different attitudes. Judges so often have the unpleasant task of passing substantial sentences of imprisonment that they may sometimes welcome an opportunity to be lenient.

As the seriousness of the offence alone was unlikely to have led to the committal decision by the magistrates, those committed could be expected to have had fairly long criminal records. Indeed, two-thirds of both London and Wessex samples had five or more previous convictions, the Wessex sample having a generally higher rate.

CONCLUSION[1]

This is the first full-scale study of the medical remand procedure and in detail goes beyond some of the excellent smaller scale studies mentioned in the Introduction. Even in such a comprehensive work as his recently completed two-volume work on *Crime and Insanity in England,* Professor Nigel Walker (1968, 1973) recognizes his inability to do justice to 'the process by which an offender is recognized as disordered by police, courts, probation officers, prison doctors or other agents of the system', and relies for his discussion on the Reports of the Prison Department and the study by Sparks (1966) of diagnostic remands in two London courts presided over by five

[1] Some of these comments have already been mentioned in Soothill and Pope's (1974) ISTD booklet, but there is a much greater opportunity to review the evidence for these conclusions in the present text.

stipendiary magistrates. Walker's conclusion is that on the evidence 'This pair of courts seems at the very least to have reached the upper limit of profitable remanding, given the *existing standards of diagnosis and treatment.*'

There has always been a considerable difference between the practice of medical remanding in London (and perhaps other large conurbations) and elsewhere. The Cambridge study (Radzinowicz, 1957) of Sexual Offenders, describing the situation in the early 1950s, noted 'in areas outside the metropolis and the large cities it is frequently difficult to obtain a medical report unless the offender was remanded in custody'. The present study shows that these differences continue but that the situation is reversed, for Wessex were better organized to deal with these problems smoothly, economically, and efficiently. Crime, especially in its more sophisticated and grossly disordered manifestations, is remarkably concentrated in the centres of large conurbations and the strains upon social organization which produce it also impose a severe burden on the social and remedial services as well as the courts. But large cities are also centres of learning and often of innovation and experiment.

A question which the present study cannot fully answer is why magistrates ask for a medical report and what they expect it to contain? To exclude the possibility of major mental illness in a serious offender liable to be sent to prison may be as important to the magistrate as to recommend treatment for those who need it. In the juvenile courts the motive for asking for a psychological report is no longer to select those who need treatment; the report is designed, with the probation report, to provide a comprehensive assessment of the social, psychological, mental, educational, and vocational situation and needs of an offender, especially if he has failed to respond to simple measures. The higher proportion of young adults aged 17–21 among London medical remands might have been because London magistrates more often wanted a comprehensive social and personality assessment than an answer to the more restricted question of whether or not psychiatric treatment is desirable. We have seen that Wessex probation officers would have found a psychiatric report useful in 18 per cent of the 'controls' (half of whom were 17–21) for whom a medical report had not been requested; this almost certainly implied psychiatric interpretation and advice about the best approach to the offender's problems—after the pattern common in juveniles—rather than referral for treatment. The value of this sort of psychiatric report is that the offender and his relatives tend to have certain attitudes to and expectations about doctors that persuade them to discuss with doctors personal, family, and marital problems which they are reluctant to discuss with others.

There remains the problem of why so many remands should be carried out in custody. Even if it is difficult to estimate the differences, if any, between the offender population in London and Wessex, all studies of those remanded in custody for these reports show that even in the London population the majority seemed suitable for examination on bail, on the criteria of not being dangerous, unlikely to co-operate, or homeless, etc.; and, in Wessex remand on bail to National Health Service consultants resulted in nearly five times as many probation orders with a condition of psychiatric treatment. Collaboration between the psychiatric service and the probation service is the most essential future development but in furthering both psychiatric and penal policy the aim is to deal with as many patients or offenders as possible at liberty, and so to advance their social integration. One of the most important results of this study has been to show that this collaboration is initiated earlier and more effectively in Wessex, by means of the pre-trial probation interview. Meanwhile, the bail clinics at Brixton and Holloway prisons, set up so that the prison medical service can provide a report on bail, have been little used—in 1975 only 90 cases out of 3,500 custodial remands.

Here too the practice with juveniles might have been of influence. A period in a remand home for juveniles with observation of behaviour in a paternalistic setting, discussion with sympathetic adults and investigation of educational or vocational assets and handicaps is constructive even though contamination and group indoctrination in delinquent habits may continue. For the great majority, however, of young adults in remand centres or adults in prison the period is spent in a cell, and amounts to a sentence of three weeks in prison, not a period of informative observation. In remand centres the drain on staff for escort duties severely limits staff observation and the effects of contamination by more experienced and cynical delinquents outweigh any positive value.

Magistrates and some psychiatrists often argue that the custodial remand 'concentrates the mind wonderfully' (as Dr. Johnson said of the death penalty). A certain type of adolescent or young adult delinquent cannot or will not appreciate the threat of the law till he actually experiences it. But it seems strange that such salutary effects, when necessary, could not be obtained by repeated remands on bail, the court saying in effect 'We are not at all satisfied that you take this offence seriously. We are thinking of sending you to detention. Come back next week and meanwhile have a talk with the probation officer.'

Medical remands by the high court judges are more difficult to interpret, since they represent only a part of the medical information reaching the court. The attitude of the more serious offender who is prepared to co-operate on bail so long as he has a hope of acquittal may change sharply on conviction. There may be a clearer division between those whom the court intends to sentence to imprisonment and those whom they propose to set at liberty, especially if psychiatric treatment is provided.

The recent Home Office *Report of the Home Office Working Party* (1974) on *Bail Procedures in Magistrates' Courts* did not make any major recommendation with regard to medical reports. Some of the early findings of this present work were made available to the Working Party but the possible implications were not considered in any detail. The Report stressed that 'remands for medical reports present magistrates with special difficulties' but failed to recognize the extent to which the probation service, for example, may be helpful in deciding whether a medical report would be useful.

With regard to custodial remands the Working Party received differing views about the value of custody and observed only that 'we are not qualified to attempt to resolve the conflicting views on an essentially medical question'. This conclusion appears to hint at a 'demarcation dispute' between the medical and other penal professions which it is in everyone's interest to break down. We hope that this study has provided supportive evidence for what we believe to be the truth—that there are *no* reasons for differentiating medical remands from any others. It is not an essentially medical question. Anyone who is suitable for remand on bail by general lay standards is suitable for remand on bail for a medical report. Laymen tend to over-estimate the 'dangers' of the mentally disordered offender because his motivations seem unintelligible. A small proportion of grossly disordered offenders undoubtedly need immediate custodial care when they first appear in court; prison hospital is always available, whereas admission to a psychiatric hospital is a lengthy, sometimes unsatisfactory, procedure. The Scottish system which allows courts to commit offenders on remand to mental hospitals, if necessary without their consent, has certain advantages.

Some of these problems will perhaps be ameliorated by the establishment in several more areas of the country of 'joint appointments' of consultant forensic psychiatrists who are part-time to both the Health Service and to the prison medical service. Often the same psychiatrist will see the offender, whether on bail or in custody, and those appointed will have knowledge of both the psychiatric resources within the prison system as well as local community and hospital resources. This will greatly improve the service especially for those who require some form of custody or institutionalization, whether in hospital, special hospital or prison. But to concentrate forensic psychiatric practice in the hands of relatively few forensic psychiatrists and their assistants would, we think, be counter-productive. The trend both in psychiatric practice and in general penal policy is to integrate or re-integrate the offender as soon and as far as possible in the community, and to resist or overcome the general tendency to regard him (and for him to regard himself) as an outcast or special case. If the great majority of offenders with psychiatric problems would be increasingly dealt with by general consultant psychiatrists or by those who have a special interest, and with the essential help of the probation service, as many as possible could be treated and supported in the community.

POSTSCRIPT

THE BUTLER REPORT

SINCE this report was prepared, the Butler Committee on Mentally Abnormal Offenders has produced its final report (H.M.S.O. Cmnd. 6244), with many detailed recommendations affecting the preparation of medical reports to court. They are very welcome and many are consonant with recommendations which follow from our findings. In summary, the recommendations relevant to this study are as follows:

(1) *Section* 136 (direct police admission to hospital) 'should continue to be used to the maximum to ensure that as many as possible of the mentally disordered offenders within the scope of the provision are referred at the outset to the treatment agencies without the need to bring them before the courts' ... 'Where any apparent offender is clearly in urgent need of psychiatric treatment and there is no question of risk to members of the public, the question should always be asked whether any useful public purpose would be served by prosecution. The medical report should be taken into account together with, where possible, a report on the circumstances by a social worker. These remarks apply in cases of homicide or grave bodily harm as in less serious cases' ... 'Prosecution ... should not be embarked upon where it is not clearly in the interests of the patient or the community.'

(2) *Information for the courts.* 'We propose that greater use should be made of social inquiry reports as a screening process for mental disorder and to indicate the need for a full psychiatric report.' Social inquiry reports should be mandatory in cases involving serious violence or danger to the person. This should include all cases of grave non-sexual offences against the person, or sexual offences on children below the age of 13 or offences involving violence to persons of any age, and property offences which involve risk to life (for example, arson).

(3) *Remands to Hospital.* There should be a form of court order giving courts the power to remand a mentally disordered person to hospital before deciding his ultimate disposal when (i) a medical report is required on a convicted defendant; (ii) the defendant requires medical care during a custodial remand; (iii) a period in hospital is required to determine whether a hospital order is appropriate; (iv) when a defendant is found under disability in relation to the trial. The order should be available at all National Health Service hospitals and the proposed regional secure units and special hospitals. The duration

should be a maximum of three months, if the remand is for medical reports or care, and in other cases if for three months initially, should be extendable by one month at a time to a maximum of six months. Remand to hospitals should be considered only if remand on bail is not feasible. The power to remand to hospital should be exercised only when there is medical evidence to suggest mental disorder and a hospital place is available. The secure custody of a remanded mentally disordered defendant will sometimes be needed; it will be for the courts to decide whether this need will be met by remand to a local psychiatric hospital or regional secure unit; or, exceptionally, to the security of a special hospital. If no suitable hospital place is available, remand to prison, though generally undesirable, may be unavoidable. All defendants remanded to hospital remain within the jurisdiction of the court.

If the recommendations about committal of those strongly suspected of mental abnormality to hospitals, either the general psychiatric hospitals or the new secure units or even the special hospitals are accepted, this may go some way to reduce the numbers of those admitted to prison, who need immediate treatment as well as control.

Among the many other important recommendations are that magistrates as well as Crown Courts should be empowered to deal with persons 'under disability' (unfit to plead) and that the test of criminal responsibility (the McNaghten Rules) should be changed. These, however, refer to the outcome of remand, rather than to the machinery of remand with which we have been concerned in this report.

The recommendations cited relate to suggestions for changes in the law or regulations, but the Committee was clearly constantly aware of the need to improve services, especially the co-ordination of different services for the examination and treatment of abnormal offenders. The Committee gave the most detailed consideration to the exact means by which legal changes might be achieved, including consideration of sections and even sub-sections of acts which would need modification. The specification of changes in the development and co-ordination of medical and social facilities was inevitably more general, though the recommendations give careful thought to the *direction* of improvement, and the policies necessary to achieve it. The recommendations, in the words of one of its members, Dr. Acres, divide clearly into those of 'the law and the prophets'. The direction of development advised by the 'prophets' is no less important than the specification of the lawyers.

In considering the question—in some ways the most difficult of all—'when should reports be prepared', the Committee concludes that the magistrates should rely largely upon the probation officers, who should be sensitive to signs of mental abnormality and obtain a history of previous psychiatric breakdown or treatment. Experienced magistrates will, of course, have additional ideas about what kind of offender would repay a psychiatric report. On this issue it will be seen that the present study strongly supports the recommendation. Although general guidance can be given to magistrates about the type of case likely to repay psychiatric examination, slavish following of 'rules' (e.g. shop-lifting by middle-aged women of previous good character') would result in far more requests for reports than the psychiatrists could provide; in most cases moreover a report would serve no purpose. There has to be selection and magistrates need to be reminded that some individuals, whatever their age, and offence, call for a report, once the social and medical history is known.

On this subject it will be remembered that our report produced the interesting finding that in spite of the smooth working system in Wessex, the probation officers reported that in 18 per cent of cases who were *not* psychiatrically examined, a report 'would probably have been helpful'. We calculated that even a small percentage of increase in reports requested under the present arrangements would probably overload the psychiatrists involved. We drew attention to this feature, that members of helping agencies, such as the probation service, tend when faced with an apparently irremediable situation, to feel that additional skilled help would succeed. They probably overestimate, especially when inexperienced, the skill and capacity of the psychiatric profession in all areas of mental disorder, especially personality disorders. As the Committee emphasized, the matter is one essentially of closer collaboration between the different services. Our study revealed that because so few consultant psychiatrists have experience of preparing psychiatric reports for the court about offenders on bail, most consultants are unaware of the capacity, expertise, and nation-wide organization of the probation service, which is by far the most efficient social service, obliged often to accept responsibility for the supervision of dangerous and grossly disordered offenders at liberty.

The Committee stressed that full information should be made available to the reporting doctor, together with the reasons for requesting the report. At present clerks of the court are requested but not legally required to provide this information. We found that no reason was given for requiring a report in 40 per cent of magistrates' cases and in the rest the reasons were expressed too generally ('No fixed abode' or 'demeanour in court') to be helpful. The prison medical officers who considered that 10 per cent of requests for a report were 'unnecessary' probably considered that the question related to manifest mental illness or gross abnormality, whereas the question was probably 'can you think of any useful form of medical or social care?' The motives of magistrates in asking for a report are very varied and constantly evolving.

One of the most important series of recommendations relates to co-ordination and co-operation between probation and psychiatric services, and between the prison medical service and National Health Service psychiatrists. The relationship of these two medical services was not within their terms of reference, we believe; but they made valuable suggestions with regard to the frequent secondment of both psychiatric registrars and prison doctors as appropriate to the prison service, special hospitals, and for work with the new consultant forensic psychiatrists' units set up in several centres, in which the consultant works part-time in the prisons and part-time in the N.H.S. An especially important suggestion was that there should be a new 'Senior Registrar' grade in the Prison Medical Service. The Forensic Sub-committee of the Royal College of Psychiatrists has the duty to lay down the range of training required of senior registrars to become eligible for eventual appointment as consultant forensic psychiatrists. In this way increasingly similar standards of training and range of experience for the different branches of forensic work could be established.

The Use of Charge Sheets as a Documentary Source in the Study of Medical Remands

WHILE no national police force exists the lack of a standardized charge sheet and uniform information recording is likely to persist. Nevertheless, the charge sheets of the Metropolitan Police for the Inner London Area contained sufficient information to form the basis of the retrospective study of medical remands, more especially as the details of each remand during an individual's progress through the courts were carefully documented. This also applied to the City of London Police but in Wessex some remand details were omitted from the charge sheets of one crucial police force and for Wessex as a whole the charge sheets had, therefore, to be discarded as an inappropriate source of data.[1]

Not each offence committed or each offender apprehended necessitates a charge sheet; the basic division is between the issuing of a summons and the arrest. It is on these latter occasions that a charge sheet is completed. The Criminal Justice Act, 1967, has laid down that a warrant for an arrest of a person who is at least 17 years old shall not be issued unless the offence to which the warrant relates is: (a) indictable; (b) punishable with imprisonment or unless the address of the defendant is not sufficiently established for a summons to be served on him.[2] Other than this no hard and fast rules govern whether a summons or arrest procedure is used. The use of the summons in Inner London is not fully documented and thus the only group that we are certain has been omitted from the medical remand group are offenders committing crimes excluded by the above criteria. The group in which we were most interested was on the whole likely to be the subject of a charge sheet, for the offences, if not indictable, were almost always imprisonable or else the defendants were of no fixed abode. Of the 46,000 or so indictable offenders brought before the courts within the Metropolitan Police District during 1969, about 300 or less than one per cent were summonsed.

As we have already said, we have no direct way of assessing the extent of our sample losses that were due to the use of the summons procedure, although one way of approaching this, as well as acquiring information about the overall completeness of the medical remand sample, is to compare the 1969 pilot study sample with the 1969 retrospective study sample. The former was collected from the remand prisons (the source of the medical report) the latter came from the charge sheets, so that the discrepancy between the two samples should give some indication of their comprehensiveness. Some 'residual' discrepancy will, of course, be due to the fact that the samples were collected from different sets of documents at different times and thus not only are there problems of sorting out medical reports to lower and higher courts but also, more mundanely, of the spelling of names and the use of aliases. It has only been possible to compare seven courts for a three-month period and thus there are

---

[1] In fairness, it must also be pointed out that this was not the whole reason for such a decision being taken. As will emerge in the following paragraphs, the use of summons in rural areas made the court registers a more comprehensive and hence more suitable source of data.

[2] Criminal Justice Act, 1967, S24 (1).

problems of 'different' courts and of the appropriate cut-off period. Although we have tried to overcome as many of these problems as possible in order to be able to undertake this comparison it must be made clear that the figures of agreement represent the *minimum* level only.

The sort of figures suggest that for a study of medical remands over several courts the charge sheets provide a fairly comprehensive source of data.

RELATIONSHIP BETWEEN 1969 PILOT
AND 1969 RETROSPECTIVE SAMPLES

Court	Age 17–21 % Agreement between samples	Age over 21 % Agreement between samples
Balham M.C.	88·9	90·9
Bow Street M.C.	91·7	90·8
Clerkenwell M.C.	95·5	89·4
Lambeth M.C.	94·1	92·0
South-Western M.C.	88·2	94·4
Thames M.C.	87·5	92·3
West London M.C.	93·7	88·9
Total	91·4	91·0

For Wessex, the problem differed for besides the lack of information on the charge sheets summons and arrest procedures were used differently.

Bottomley's study (1970) of court practices noted an important division in that 'as many as one fifth of the rural cases were summonsed, whereas in the urban sample less than 2 per cent were proceeded against by summons'. The advantage and greater use of the summons within rural areas derive from the fact that rural courts sit relatively infrequently as compared with their urban counterparts and small 'single-manned' police stations have limited provisions for detaining offenders overnight and bringing them before a magistrate within 24 hours. Any assessment of the relative advantages or uses of the summons and arrest procedures was beyond the scope of the present research, but the implications of Bottomley's findings for the Wessex area are clear. If the charge sheets had been the sole source of data, one of the central reasons for choosing to study the Wessex region with its continuum of urban and rural courts would have been negated, for certain medical remands in the rural areas may result from a summons and no charge sheet would have been made out.

Different sources of data for Inner London and Wessex, it could be argued, make the sample not strictly comparable. However, if the charge sheets had been adopted for both samples, then in one area considerable information would be lacking about the medical remands, and a systematic and serious bias would also have been introduced into the assessment of medical remands in rural courts. On the other hand, if the court registers had been used exclusively, not only would the speed of collection and the comprehensiveness of the Inner London sample have suffered but the use of the London court registers as sources of information would have raised problems.

In the final event, we believe that the use of the two sources of information has been justified not only in minimizing the bias between the samples but also in maximizing the returns of medical remands. On those occasions where the information for the two samples is not comparable this has been pointed out.

APPENDIX 2

Questionnaire completed by Hospital Consultants and Prison Medical Officers

STUDY ON MEDICAL REPORTS TO THE COURTS

With a grant from the Home Office Research Unit, the Institute of Psychiatry is studying under the direction of Professor T. C. N. Gibbens, the role of psychiatric facilities in the penal setting. This particular project is concerned with medical reports presented to the criminal courts.

This project is concerned with persons aged 17 and over and the aim is for one of these forms to be completed for *every* person for whom a report is presented to a court in the Wessex Regional Hospital Board Area after 1st September, 1970. In effect, the Wessex Area covers all the courts in Hampshire, Dorset and South Wiltshire (a list of the relevant courts is given in alphabetical order on page 2).

We hope that you feel able to co-operate in this study and that the extra work involved will not prove too burdensome.

IF YOU HAVE ANY QUERIES OR PROBLEMS ON THIS QUESTIONNAIRE, PLEASE CONTACT:-

> Keith Soothill
> Forensic Psychiatry,
> 119 Camberwell Road,
> London, S.E.5
> Tel: 01-703-5501/2

TO BE COMPLETED BY DOCTOR

CONSULTANT QUESTIONNAIRE

FULL NAME OF SUBJECT ....

AGE ....   DATE OF BIRTH (IF KNOWN) ....

PLEASE TICK ☑ APPROPRIATE BOX

INVOLVED IN THE CASE BECAUSE:

DIRECT REQUEST BY ☐   DIRECT REQUEST BY ☐   DEFENCE PURPOSES ☐
MAGISTRATES' COURT   HIGHER COURT

REQUEST BY A HOSPITAL ☐   REQUEST BY A PRISON ☐   VOLUNTARY REPORT ☐
DOCTOR FOR A SECOND   DOCTOR FOR A SECOND
OPINION (e.g. for   OPINION (e.g. for
S.60 purpose)   S.60 purpose)

OTHER ☐   Please specify ....

WHICH COURT WILL RECEIVE THIS REPORT ? ....

WHERE DID YOU INTERVIEW THIS MAN ? ....

DATE OF INTERVIEW ....

ESTIMATE OF TOTAL TIME SPENT IN DEALING WITH THIS SUBJECT (INCLUDE TRAVELLING
TIMES, ETC. BUT DISREGARD TIME SPENT COMPLETING THIS QUESTIONNAIRE)
            ....hours   .... minutes

IF SUBJECT WAS SEEN IN CUSTODY, WAS THIS THE SOLE PURPOSE OF YOUR VISIT ?

YES ☐   PRIMARY PURPOSE ☐   ONE OF SEVERAL ☐

The following list gives the courts in which we are interested:

HAMPSHIRE		DORSET	WILTSHIRE
Aldershot	Kingsclere	Blandford	Amesbury
Alresford	Lymington	Bridport	Mere
Alton	Newport (I.O.W.)	Dorchester	Salisbury
Andover	Odiham	Gillingham	Tisbury
Basingstoke	Petersfield	Lyme Regis	
Bournemouth	Portsmouth	Poole	
Christchurch	Ringwood	Portland	
Droxford	Romsey	Shaftesbury	
Eastleigh	Southampton	Sherborne	
Fareham	Totton	Sturminster	
Gosport	Winchester	Swanage	
Havant		Wareham	
Hythe		Weymouth	
		Wimborne	

HIGHER COURTS. Include all cases from quarter sessions held in any of the
above towns and include all cases from Hampshire, Dorset and Wiltshire Assizes.

TO BE COMPLETED BY THE DOCTOR
PLEASE TICK ☑ APPROPRIATE BOX

We would be grateful if you would complete the following pages for this case:

Page 3 (this page) deals with the physical and psychiatric history.
Page 4 asks for your opinion on a few matters.
Page 5 asks you to make an assessment on a number of different factors and on the back of it there are some notes which may be helpful to you.
Page 6 asks for your recommendations to court.

NAME OF SUBJECT ....

PHYSICAL HEALTH

DOES THE SUBJECT REGARD PHYSICAL ILL-HEALTH OR DISABILITY A PROBLEM?

VERY MUCH SO ☐   SLIGHTLY ☐   NOT AT ALL ☐   DON'T KNOW ☐

Please give brief details ....

IN YOUR OPINION IS PHYSICAL ILL-HEALTH OR DISABILITY A PROBLEM FOR THE SUBJECT?

VERY MUCH SO ☐   SLIGHTLY ☐   NOT AT ALL ☐   DON'T KNOW ☐

Please give brief details ....

ANY CONTACT WITH GENERAL HOSPITAL FOR PHYSICAL PROBLEMS?

WITHIN LAST YEAR ☐   WITHIN LAST 5 YEARS ☐   OVER 5 YEARS ☐   NO EVIDENCE ☐

* Please note last two hospitals with appropriate dates and also give reasons for contact:

1) ....
2) ....

PSYCHIATRIC HISTORY

ANY CONTACT WITH HOSPITAL AS IN-PATIENT OR OUT-PATIENT FOR PSYCHIATRIC PROBLEMS?

WITHIN LAST YEAR ☐   WITHIN LAST 5 YEARS ☐   OVER 5 YEARS ☐   NO EVIDENCE ☐

* Please note last two hospitals with appropriate dates stating whether in- or out-patient:

1) ....
2) ....

WAS HE STILL ATTENDING ANY OF THE ABOVE HOSPITALS FOR ANY REASON IN THE MONTH PRIOR TO HIS COURT APPEARANCE?   YES ☐   NO ☐

IF YES, WHICH HOSPITAL? ....

* The purpose of these questions is to gain sufficient information for us to be able to contact at a later date the hospitals for their case records.

YOUR OPINION (PLEASE ANSWER FOR ALL MEN)

WHICH IN YOUR ESTIMATION WAS THE MOST LIKELY REASON FOR THE DEMAND FOR A MEDICAL REPORT ON THIS MAN? (Disregard this question for defence or voluntary reports to court.)

PATIENT APPEARED ILL AT COURT HEARING ☐
COURT HAD KNOWLEDGE OF PREVIOUS MENTAL HEALTH ☐
NATURE OF PRESENT OFFENCE ☐
COURT ADDED MEDICAL TO OTHER ENQUIRIES FOR GOOD MEASURE ☐
COURT FELT THAT TASTE OF PRISON MAY ACT AS WARNING ☐
OTHER NON-MEDICAL REASONS (e.g. solicitor, defendant, probation request) ....

IN YOUR OPINION WAS THE REQUEST A REASONABLE ONE?

YES ☐   NO ☐   UNDECIDED ☐

IN THINKING OF THIS MAN'S RELATIONSHIPS WITH HIS CONTEMPORARIES, WOULD YOU SUSPECT THAT:

| HE IS A LONE WOLF ☐ | HE MIXED MAINLY WITH A DEVIANT ☐ GROUP (e.g. 'drug culture', 'criminal gang') | HE MIXES MAINLY WITH NON-DEVIANTS ☐ | DON'T KNOW ☐ |

IN HIS DISCUSSION WITH YOU, DID HE SHOW ANY SIGNS OF:

SULLENNESS	YES ☐	NO ☐
HOSTILITY	YES ☐	NO ☐
FRIENDLINESS	YES ☐	NO ☐
ANXIETY	YES ☐	NO ☐
WILLINGNESS TO DISCUSS HIS PROBLEMS	YES ☐	NO ☐

IF IT WERE NECESSARY, WOULD THIS MAN IN YOUR OPINION BE LIKELY TO FOLLOW A COURSE OF OUT-PATIENT TREATMENT (i.e. IN TERMS OF KEEPING APPOINTMENTS, ETC.)

VERY RELIABLE ☐   FAIRLY RELIABLE ☐   DEFINITELY UNRELIABLE ☐

IN COMPILING THE MEDICAL REPORT FOR THE COURT, WERE THERE ANY PARTICULAR DIFFICULTIES WHICH MADE YOUR TASK HARDER IN ASSESSING THIS MAN? (e.g. previous hospital failed to supply past records in time, no psychologist available to administer suitable tests, etc.).

....
....
....
....
....

WAS A PROBATION REPORT OF USE TO YOU IN THIS CASE?

YES ☐   NO ☐   NOT SEEN ☐

THE CLASSIFICATION OF MEN REMANDED FOR A MEDICAL REPORT

Please tick each classification in the appropriate column, according to the way you would assess the respondent's problems at the time of interviewing him.

Please make sure that you place one tick against each factor; you may find the notes overleaf helpful.

I. BASIC PERSONALITY OR LIFE-STYLE	ABSENT	MILD	MODERATE	SEVERE	DON'T KNOW
Immature personality					
Mental retardation					
Character deficiency					
Mood swings					

II. PRESENT MENTAL STATE	ABSENT	MILD	MODERATE	SEVERE	DON'T KNOW
Anxiety state					
Depression					
Other Neurotic Symptoms					
Psychosis					
Dementia					

If any of the above in section II was markedly different at time of the offence, please comment.

....

....

III. PROBLEM AREAS

ALCOHOL: NO SERIOUS PROBLEM ☐ REPEATED DRINKER ☐ CHRONIC ALCOHOLIC ☐
    AT TIME OF OFFENCE: HAD BEEN DRINKING ☐ NO EVIDENCE OF DRINKING ☐

DRUGS: NON-USER ☐   USER (MAIN TYPE OF DRUG) ....
    DEGREE OF USE: INTERMITTENT ☐   REGULAR ☐   ADDICTED ☐

OTHER PROBLEM AREAS. (Please use this to add anything you consider relevant which may not be included in a probation officer's report, e.g. epilepsy, sex deviation.)

....
....
....
....
....
....
.... If you need extra space please use facing page.

NOTES ON THE CLASSIFICATION

On the previous page you are asked to assess men remanded for a medical report on a number of different factors. It is hoped that the following notes, while not definitive, may be of use to you in making your assessment.

I. BASIC PERSONALITY OR LIFE-STYLE

The following groups include persons who show an inability to cope with normal demands of life due to a deficiency or retardation of personal development.

Immature personality: These persons are characterized by attitudes and feelings appropriate to a lower chronological age. They are slow in growing up and in assuming responsibility. Generally, they are self-centred, demanding and dependent. (Physical immaturity alone should not be regarded as 'immature personality'.)

Mental Retardation: This category concerns the functional assessment of a person's intellectual development rather than a specific categorization in terms of his I.Q. level. The 'severe' category may be conceptualized as being relevant when there is serious consideration given to the suitability of placing such a person in a hospital for sub-normals. The 'moderate' category is appropriate when it may be said of such a person that he 'lacks judgement and discrimination' yet the aptness of placing him in a hospital for sub-normals is hardly considered. The 'mild' category is apt when it may be said that although a person suffers from some intellectual impairment this does not amount to a case for treatment as a sub-normal. Such individuals may be characterized as 'dim' or 'dull', 'inert and passive, easily fooled, credulous'.

Character Deficiency: These persons appear to have little conscience, not feeling much conscious guilt. They are often in trouble appearing unable to profit from experience or punishment. They lack a sense of loyalty or responsibility, and are plausible and try to manipulate people.

Mood Swings: Under this heading are included those conditions in which noticeable mood swings occur but the 'mild' and 'moderate' categories do not necessarily amount to a clinical diagnosis of an affective disorder. (Classify a clinical diagnosis of 'mood swings' under 'severe'.)

II. PRESENT MENTAL STATE

These five categories relate to the clinical categorization of the patient at the time of interview.

Anxiety State: Code as 'severe' where anxiety is the primary and dominant part of the clinical picture.

Depression: Classify under this heading Depressive Illness/Symptoms of both Reactive and Endogenous aetiologies.

Other Neurotic Symptoms: Include here other psychoneurotic conditions, e.g. Hysteria, phobias, obsessional states, not included elsewhere.

Psychosis: Within the limitation of the concept of 'psychosis' this category includes schizophrenia, and psychoses associated with cerebral and physical conditions. However, you will note that psychosis associated with dementia and endogenous depression are to be coded separately.

Dementia: This category includes Primary degenerative conditions (Senile, Pre-Senile Dementia, Pick's Disease, Huntingdon's Chorea, etc.) as well as certain cardiovascular disorders (Arteriosclerotic Dementia).

RECOMMENDATIONS TO COURT

Please attach a copy of the medical report you have written for the court. If this is available, please disregard the rest of this page.

FORMAL RECOMMENDATIONS (i.e. within the meaning of the various acts).

INFORMAL RECOMMENDATIONS (e.g. comments or suggestions about possible ways that the court may wish to deal with the patient).

SIGNATURE ....   DATE ....

THANK YOU FOR HELPING US

CONFIDENTIAL

REMANDS FOR MEDICAL REPORTS BY THE COURTS

With a grant from the Home Office Research Unit, the Institute of Psychiatry is studying under the direction of Professor T. C. N. Gibbens, the use by the courts of remands for medical reports. We are interested in what happens in the court setting and also in discovering some basic social and medical information on those remanded for a report. The attached questionnaire is an attempt to gather systematic information on some medical aspects.

This project is concerned with persons aged 17 and over and the aim is for one of these forms to be completed for *every* person remanded for a medical report, by courts in the Wessex Regional Hospital Board Area.

We would be most grateful if a hospital officer would complete the items on page 2 for each person remanded for a medical report by courts in the Wessex Region after 1st September, 1970. A list of the relevant courts is given in alphabetical order on page 2. After completion, please pass on the questionnaire to the appropriate doctor who is preparing the report for the court. We would appreciate if the doctor could complete pages 3, 4, 5 and 6 (the pink sheets) each time. Please return the questionnaire to the hospital officer. We hope that the extra work involved will not prove too burdensome.

Thank you for helping us.

IF YOU HAVE ANY QUERIES OR PROBLEMS ON THIS QUESTIONNAIRE PLEASE CONTACT:

> Keith Soothill,
> Forensic Psychiatry,
> 119 Camberwell Road,
> London, S.E.5
> Tel: 01-703-5501/2

TO BE COMPLETED BY THE HOSPITAL OFFICER

FULL NAME OF SUBJECT: ....

AGE .... DATE OF BIRTH (IF KNOWN) ....

PRISON NO.: ....

HOSPITAL CASE PAPER NO.: ....

COURT REQUESTING MEDICAL REPORT: ....

DATE OF REQUEST: ....

DATE OF NEXT COURT APPEARANCE: ....

DOCTOR WRITING PRESENT MEDICAL REPORT: DR: ....

IF KNOWN   PREVIOUS H.C.P. NOS.: ....

                C.R.O. NO.: ....

The following list gives the courts in which we are interested. In effect it is all the courts in Hampshire, Dorset and South Wiltshire.

HAMPSHIRE		DORSET	WILTSHIRE
Aldershot	Lymington	Blandford	Amesbury
Alresford	Newport (I.O.W.)	Bridport	Mere
Alton	Odiham	Dorchester	Salisbury
Andover	Petersfield	Gillingham	Tisbury
Basingstoke	Portsmouth	Lyme Regis	
Bournemouth	Ringwood	Poole	
Christchurch	Romsey	Portland	
Droxford	Southampton	Shaftesbury	
Eastleigh	Totton	Sherborne	
Fareham	Winchester	Sturminster	
Gosport		Swanage	
Havant		Wareham	
Hythe		Weymouth	
Kingsclere		Wimborne	

HIGHER COURTS   Include all cases from quarter sessions held in any of the above towns and include all cases from Hampshire, Dorset and Wiltshire Assizes.

TO BE COMPLETED BY THE DOCTOR

PLEASE TICK ☑ APPROPRIATE BOX

We would be grateful if you would complete the following pages for this case:

Page 3 (this page) deals with the physical and psychiatric history.
Page 4 asks for your opinion on a few matters.
Page 5 asks you to make an assessment on a number of different factors and on the back of it there are some notes which may be helpful to you.
Page 6 asks for your recommendations to court.

NAME OF SUBJECT ....

PHYSICAL HEALTH

DOES THE SUBJECT REGARD PHYSICAL ILL-HEALTH OR DISABILITY A PROBLEM?

VERY MUCH SO ☐   SLIGHTLY ☐   NOT AT ALL ☐   DON'T KNOW ☐

Please give brief details ....

IN YOUR OPINION IS PHYSICAL ILL-HEALTH OR DISABILITY A PROBLEM FOR THE SUBJECT?

VERY MUCH SO ☐   SLIGHTLY ☐   NOT AT ALL ☐   DON'T KNOW ☐

Please give brief details ....

ANY CONTACT WITH GENERAL HOSPITAL FOR PHYSICAL PROBLEMS?

WITHIN LAST YEAR ☐   WITHIN LAST 5 YEARS ☐   OVER 5 YEARS ☐   NO EVIDENCE ☐

* Please note last two hospitals with appropriate dates and also give reasons for contact:

1) ....
2) ....

PSYCHIATRIC HISTORY

ANY CONTACT WITH HOSPITAL AS IN-PATIENT OR OUT-PATIENT FOR PSYCHIATRIC PROBLEMS?

WITHIN LAST YEAR ☐   WITHIN LAST 5 YEARS ☐   OVER 5 YEARS ☐   NO EVIDENCE ☐

* Please note last two hospitals with appropriate dates stating whether in- or out-patient:

1) ....
2) ....

WAS HE STILL ATTENDING ANY OF THE ABOVE HOSPITALS FOR ANY REASON IN THE MONTH PRIOR TO HIS COURT APPEARANCE?   YES ☐   NO ☐

IF YES, WHICH HOSPITAL? ....

* The purpose of these questions is to gain sufficient information for us to be able to contact at a later date the hospitals for their case records.

YOUR OPINION (PLEASE ANSWER FOR ALL MEN)

WHICH IN YOUR ESTIMATION WAS THE MOST LIKELY REASON FOR THE DEMAND FOR A MEDICAL REPORT ON THIS MAN? (Disregard this question for defence or voluntary reports to court.)

PATIENT APPEARED ILL AT COURT HEARING ☐
COURT HAD KNOWLEDGE OF PREVIOUS MENTAL HEALTH ☐
NATURE OF PRESENT OFFENCE ☐
COURT ADDED MEDICAL TO OTHER ENQUIRIES FOR GOOD MEASURE ☐
COURT FELT THAT TASTE OF PRISON MAY ACT AS WARNING ☐
OTHER NON-MEDICAL REASONS (e.g. solicitor, defendant, probation request) ....

IN YOUR OPINION WAS THE REQUEST A REASONABLE ONE?

YES ☐   NO ☐   UNDECIDED ☐

IN THINKING OF THIS MAN'S RELATIONSHIPS WITH HIS CONTEMPORARIES, WOULD YOU SUSPECT THAT:

| HE IS A LONE WOLF ☐ | HE MIXED MAINLY WITH A DEVIANT ☐ GROUP (e.g. 'drug culture', 'criminal gang') | HE MIXES MAINLY WITH NON-DEVIANTS ☐ | DON'T KNOW ☐ |

IN HIS DISCUSSION WITH YOU, DID HE SHOW ANY SIGNS OF:

SULLENNESS	YES ☐	NO ☐
HOSTILITY	YES ☐	NO ☐
FRIENDLINESS	YES ☐	NO ☐
ANXIETY	YES ☐	NO ☐
WILLINGNESS TO DISCUSS HIS PROBLEMS	YES ☐	NO ☐

IF IT WERE NECESSARY, WOULD THIS MAN IN YOUR OPINION BE LIKELY TO FOLLOW A COURSE OF OUT-PATIENT TREATMENT (i.e. IN TERMS OF KEEPING APPOINTMENTS, ETC.)

VERY RELIABLE ☐   FAIRLY RELIABLE ☐   DEFINITELY UNRELIABLE ☐

IN COMPILING THE MEDICAL REPORT FOR THE COURT, WERE THERE ANY PARTICULAR DIFFICULTIES WHICH MADE YOUR TASK HARDER IN ASSESSING THIS MAN? (e.g. previous hospital failed to supply past records in time, no psychologist available to administer suitable tests, etc.).

....
....
....
....
....

WAS A PROBATION REPORT OF USE TO YOU IN THIS CASE?

YES ☐   NO ☐   NOT SEEN ☐

THE CLASSIFICATION OF MEN REMANDED FOR A MEDICAL REPORT

Please tick each classification in the appropriate column, according to the way you would assess the respondent's problems at the time of interviewing him.

Please make sure that you place one tick against each factor; you may find the notes overleaf helpful.

I. BASIC PERSONALITY OR LIFE-STYLE	ABSENT	MILD	MODERATE	SEVERE	DON'T KNOW
Immature personality					
Mental retardation					
Character deficiency					
Mood swings					

II. PRESENT MENTAL STATE	ABSENT	MILD	MODERATE	SEVERE	DON'T KNOW
Anxiety state					
Depression					
Other Neurotic Symptoms					
Psychosis					
Dementia					

If any of the above in section II was markedly different at time of the offence, please comment.

. . . .

. . . .

III. PROBLEM AREAS

ALCOHOL: NO SERIOUS PROBLEM ☐ REPEATED DRINKER ☐ CHRONIC ALCOHOLIC ☐

AT TIME OF OFFENCE: HAD BEEN DRINKING ☐ NO EVIDENCE OF DRINKING ☐

DRUGS: NON-USER ☐   USER (MAIN TYPE OF DRUG) . . . .

DEGREE OF USE: INTERMITTENT ☐ REGULAR ☐ ADDICTED ☐

OTHER PROBLEM AREAS. (Please use this to add anything you consider relevant which may not be included in a probation officer's report, e.g. epilepsy, sex deviation.)

. . . .

. . . .

. . . .

. . . .

. . . .

. . . .

. . . . If you need extra space please use facing page.

NOTES ON THE CLASSIFICATION (*see overleaf*)

On the previous page you are asked to assess men remanded for a medical report on a number of different factors. It is hoped that the following notes, while not definitive, may be of use to you in making your assessment.

I. BASIC PERSONALITY OR LIFE-STYLE

The following groups include persons who show an inability to cope with normal demands of life due to a deficiency or retardation of personal development.

Immature personality: These persons are characterized by attitudes and feelings appropriate to a lower chronological age. They are slow in growing up and in assuming responsibility. Generally, they are self-centred, demanding and dependant. (Physical immaturity alone should not be regarded as 'immature personality'.)

Mental Retardation: This category concerns the functional assessment of a person's intellectual development rather than a specific categorization in terms of his I.Q. level. The 'severe' category may be conceptualized as being relevant when there is serious consideration given to the suitability of placing such a person in a hospital for sub-normals. The 'moderate' category is appropriate when it may be said of such a person that he 'lacks judgement and discrimination' yet the aptness of placing him in a hospital for sub-normals is hardly considered. The 'mild' category is apt when it may be said that although a person suffers from some intellectual impairment this does not amount to a case for treatment as a sub-normal. Such individuals may be characterized as 'dim' or 'dull', 'inert and passive, easily fooled, credulous'.

Character Deficiency: These persons appear to have little conscience, not feeling much conscious guilt. They are often in trouble, appearing unable to profit from experience or punishment. They lack a sense of loyalty or responsibility, and are plausible and try to manipulate people.

Mood Swings: Under this heading are included those conditions in which noticeable mood swings occur but the 'mild' and 'moderate' categories do not necessarily amount to a clinical diagnosis of an affective disorder. (Classify a clinical diagnosis of 'mood swings' under 'severe'.)

II. PRESENT MENTAL STATE

These five categories relate to the clinical categorization of the patient at the time of interview.

Anxiety State: Code as 'severe' where anxiety is the primary and dominant part of the clinical picture.

Depression: Classify under this heading Depressive Illness/Symptoms of both Reactive and Endogenous aetiologies.

Other Neurotic Symptoms: Include here other psychoneurotic conditions, e.g. Hysteria, phobias, obsessional states, not included elsewhere.

Psychosis: Within the limitation of the concept of 'psychosis' this category includes schizophrenia, and psychoses associated with cerebral and physical conditions. However, you will note that psychosis associated with dementia and endogenous depression are to be coded separately.

Dementia: This category includes Primary degenerative conditions (Senile, Pre-Senile Dementia, Pick's Disease, Huntingdon's Chorea, etc.) as well as certain cardiovascular disorders (Arteriosclerotic Dementia).

RECOMMENDATIONS TO COURT

Please attach a copy of the medical report you have written for the court. If this is available, please disregard the rest of this page.

FORMAL RECOMMENDATIONS (i.e. within the meaning of the various acts).

INFORMAL RECOMMENDATIONS (e.g. comments or suggestions about possible ways that the court may wish to deal with the patient).

SIGNATURE ....   DATE ....

THANK YOU FOR HELPING US

Total Time from First Court Appearance to Date of Sentence for Inner London (1969) Sample

	Male		Female		Total	
	No.	%	No.	%	No.	%
0–8 days	137	4·1	36	5·5	173	4·4
9–15 days	912	27·6	165	25·4	1,077	27·2
16–22 days	913	27·6	168	25·8	1,081	27·3
23–9 days	382	11·5	86	13·2	468	11·8
30–6 days	239	7·2	43	6·6	282	7·1
37–43 days	221	6·7	38	5·8	259	6·5
44–50 days	169	5·1	23	3·5	192	4·9
51–71 days	216	6·5	45	6·9	261	6·6
Over 72 days (sentenced at Magistrates' Court)	71	2·1	23	3·5	94	2·4
Over 72 days (sentenced at Higher Court)	31	0·9	2	0·3	33	0·8
Incomplete information*	19	0·6	21	3·2	40	1·0
Total	3,310	100·0	650	100·0	3,960	100·0

* The category largely refers to cases where a 'non-appearance' after a period on bail is the last known information.

Number and Proportion of Inner London (1969) Sample Held in Custody Throughout Court Process

	Total in Sample	No. in Custody Throughout Court Process	% in Custody Throughout
0–8 days	173	173	100·0
9–15 days	1,077	1,048	97·3
16–22 days	1,081	969	89·7
23–9 days	468	242	51·7
30–6 days	282	144	51·1
37–43 days	259	98	37·8
44–50 days	192	70	36·5
51–71 days	261	81	31·0
Over 72 days (sentenced at Magistrates' Court)	94	2	2·1
Over 72 days (sentenced at Higher Court)	33	11	33·3
Incomplete information	40	9	22·5
Total	3,960	2,847	71·9

Comparison of Inner London and Wessex Areas in Terms of the Sentence of The Court (1969 Samples)

	Males		Females	
	Inner London %	*Wessex* %	*Inner London* %	*Wessex* %
Discharged, Withdrawn, Adj Sine Die	1·7	0·2	2·3	0·0
Non-Custodial Sentences				
Absolute, Conditional Discharge, Bound Over	14·6	6·1	19·6	11·7
Fines	13·5	13·1	11·2	13·0
Suspended Sentence	16·7	11·4	10·6	7·8
Probation Order	18·2	25·4	34·0	37·7
Custodial Sentences				
Detention Centre, Borstal, Attendance Centre, D.C. Recall, Borstal Recall	11·6	5·8	2·9	0·0
Total of up to 3 months Imprisonment	3·8	4·4	2·6	3·9
Total of over 3 months Imprisonment	11·7	11·9	4·5	3·9
Medical Disposals				
Psychiatric Probation Order (S.4 CJA 1948)	2·6	13·6	4·5	18·2
Hospital Order (Section 60 MHA 1959)	5·2	8·3	5·2	2·6
No Information	0·4	0·0	2·6	1·3
Total (per cent)	100·0	100·0	100·0	100·0
Total (persons)	3,310	413	650	77

Inner London versus Wessex

Males:

Medical Disposals *v.* Others: $\chi^2 = 88\cdot0$ l.d.f. significant at 0·1 per cent level
Non-Custodial Disposals *v.* Others: $\chi^2 = 7\cdot7$ l.d.f. significant at 1 per cent level
Custodial Disposals *v.* Others: $\chi^2 = 5\cdot0$ l.d.f. significant at 5 per cent level

Females:

Medical Disposals *v.* Others: $\chi^2 = 8\cdot6$ l.d.f. significant at 1·0 per cent level
Non-Custodial Disposals *v.* Others: $\chi^2 = 1\cdot0$ l.d.f. N.S. level
Custodial Disposals *v.* Others: $\chi^2 = 10\cdot4$ l.d.f. N.S.

Present Mental State of Wessex (1970–1) Sample
(*Ratings of the psychiatrists to each of five items*)

	Males		Females	
	No.	%	No.	%
Anxiety State				
Severe	3	1·2	0	—
Moderate	20	7·8	8	18·6
Mild	69	27·0	12	27·9
Absent	134	52·3	20	46·5
Don't know	0	—	0	—
No information	30	11·7	3	7·0
Total	256	100·0	43	100·0
Depression				
Severe	1	0·4	0	—
Moderate	15	5·9	7	16·3
Mild	48	18·7	13	30·2
Absent	164	64·1	19	44·2
Don't know	0	—	0	—
No information	28	10·9	4	9·3
Total	256	100·0	43	100·0
Other Neurotic Symptoms				
Severe	13	5·1	2	4·7
Moderate	18	7·0	4	9·3
Mild	25	9·8	5	11·6
Absent	162	63·3	29	67·4
Don't know	4	1·6	0	—
No information	34	13·3	3	7·0
Total	256	100·0	43	100·0
Psychosis				
Severe	9	3·5	0	—
Moderate	9	3·5	0	—
Mild	2	0·8	0	—
Absent	192	75·0	39	90·7
Don't know	4	1·6	0	—
No information	40	15·6	4	9·3
Total	256	100·0	43	100·0
Dementia				
Severe	0	—	0	—
Moderate	1	0·4	1	2·3
Mild	2	0·8	0	—
Absent	210	82·0	36	83·7
Don't know	2	0·8	0	—
No information	41	16·0	6	14·0
Total	256	100·0	43	100·0

N.B. The rating scale consisted in each case of five alternatives—severe, moderate, mild, absent, or don't know. (The questionnaire is shown fully as Appendix 2—the five items are notoriously difficult to define but the notes which were added to the questionnaire for guidance indicate the types of mental illnesses we were hoping to detect.)

Basic Personality or Life-Style of Wessex (1970–1) Sample
(*Ratings of the psychiatrists to each of four items*)

	Males		Females	
	No.	%	*No.*	%
Immature Personality				
Severe	33	12·9	8	18·6
Moderate	68	26·6	13	30·2
Mild	54	21·1	13	30·2
Absent	72	28·1	8	18·6
Don't know	2	0·8	0	—
No information	27	10·5	1	2·4
Total	256	100·0	43	100·0
Mental Retardation				
Severe	6	2·3	1	2·3
Moderate	13	5·1	6	14·0
Mild	16	6·3	6	14·0
Absent	184	71·9	26	60·4
Don't know	1	0·4	0	—
No information	36	14·1	4	9·3
Total	256	100·0	43	100·0
Character Deficiency				
Severe	25	9·8	7	16·3
Moderate	59	23·0	13	30·2
Mild	61	23·8	13	30·2
Absent	76	29·7	7	16·3
Don't know	3	1·2	0	—
No information	32	12·5	3	7·0
Total	256	100·0	43	100·0
Mood Swings				
Severe	5	2·0	3	7·0
Moderate	25	9·8	6	14·0
Mild	31	12·1	12	27·9
Absent	138	53·9	18	41·9
Don't know	13	5·1	1	2·2
No information	44	17·2	3	7·0
Total	256	100·0	43	100·0

N.B. The rating scale consisted in each case of five alternatives—severe, moderate, mild, absent or don't know. (The questionnaire is shown fully as Appendix 2—the four items used to try to delineate the basic personality are problematical, but the notes which had been adapted from Martin Davies' (1969) *Probationers in their social environment* and added to the questionnaire for guidance indicate the types of problems we wished to consider under the general heading of 'basic personality or life-style'.)

APPENDIX 8

Relationship Between Mental Health Assessment and Court Sentence

Mental Health Summary Assessment	Non-Custodial Sentences No. %		Medical Sentences* No. %		Custodial Sentences No. %		No Information No. %		Total No. %	
Males										
No problems	10	7·0	1	2·3	8	13·8	0	—	19	7·4
Mild problems only	47	32·9	4	9·1	7	12·1	1	9·1	59	23·0
Moderate personality problems	32	22·4	4	9·1	23	39·7	6	54·5	65	25·4
Moderate mental illness	4	2·8	5	11·4	0	—	0	—	9	3·5
Moderate personality and moderate mental illness	10	7·0	8	18·2	3	5·2	0	—	21	8·2
Severe personality problems	18	12·6	5	11·4	8	13·8	1	9·1	32	12·5
Severe mental illness	0	—	3	6·8	0	—	1	9·1	4	1·6
Severe mental illness and moderate personality problem	3	2·0	7	15·9	2	3·4	0	—	12	4·7
Severe personality and moderate mental illness	6	4·2	4	9·1	2	3·4	2	18·2	14	5·5
Severe personality and severe mental illness	6	4·2	3	6·8	0	—	0	—	9	3·5
No information	7	4·9	0	—	5	8·6	0	—	12	4·7
Total	143	100·0	44	100·0	58	100·0	11	100·0	256	100·0
Females										
No problems	0	—	0	—	0	—	0	—	0	—
Mild problems only	7	25·9	2	25·0	3	50·0	0	—	12	27·9
Moderate personality problems	7	25·9	2	25·0	1	16·7	2	100·0	12	27·9
Moderate mental illness	2	7·4	0	—	0	—	0	—	2	4·6
Moderate personality and moderate mental illness	2	7·4	1	12·5	0	—	0	—	3	7·0
Severe personality problem	3	11·1	2	25·0	1	16·7	0	—	6	14·0
Severe mental illness	1	3·7	0	—	0	—	0	—	1	2·3
Severe mental illness and moderate personality problem	1	3·7	0	—	0	—	0	—	1	2·3
Severe personality and moderate mental illness	4	14·8	1	12·5	1	16·7	0	—	6	14·0
Severe personality and severe mental illness	0	—	0	—	0	—	0	—	0	—
No information	0	—	0	—	0	—	0	—	0	—
Total	27	100·0	8	100·0	6	100·0	2	100·0	43	100·0

* 'Medical sentences' refer to hospital orders (section 60 Mental Health Act, 1959) and psychiatric probation orders (section 4 Criminal Justice Act, 1948).

N.B. The Mental Health Summary Assessment is an attempt to combine the two aspects of present mental state and basic personality or life-style. The procedure followed was to take the highest (i.e. the most severe) category within each group.

REFERENCES

BITTNER, E. (1967). Police discretion in emergency apprehension of mentally ill persons, *Social Problems*, **14**.

BITTNER, E. (1967). The police on skid-row: a study of peace keeping, *Amer. sociol. Rev.*, **32**.

BORRIE, G. (1971). Courts Act—a guide, *New Society*, 30 December.

BOTTOMLEY, A. K. (1970). *Prison before trial*, Occasional Papers on Social Administration, No. 39, London.

BUTLER COMMITTEE (1975). *Report of Committee on Mentally Abnormal Offenders*, Cmnd. 6244, H.M.S.O.

DAVIES, C. (1969). Imprisonment without sentence, *New Society*, 27 March.

DAVIES, M. (1969). *Probationers in their Social Environment*, Home Office Research Studies, No. 2, H.M.S.O.

DE BERKER, P. (1960). State of Mind reports: the inadequate personality, *Brit. J. Criminol.*, **1**, 1.

DELL, S. (1971). *Silent in Court*, Occasional Papers on Social Administration, No. 42, London.

DELL, S. AND GIBBENS, T. C. N. (1971). Remands of women offenders for medical reports, *Med. Sci. Law*, **11**, 117–27.

FAULK, M. AND TRAFFORD, P. A. (1975). The efficacy of medical remands, *Med. Sci. Law*, **15**, 4, 276–9.

GEORGE, H. R. (1972). *A Study of Police Admissions to Psychiatric Hospitals*, M.D. Thesis, University of London.

GIBBENS, T. C. N. (1963). *Psychiatric Studies of Borstal Lads*, Maudsley Monograph, No. 11, London.

GIBBENS, T. C. N. AND SILBERMAN, M. (1970). Alcoholism among prisoners, *Psychol. Med.*, **1**, 73–8.

GIBSON, E. (1960). *Time Spent Awaiting Trial*, Studies in the Causes of Delinquency and the Treatment of Offenders, No. 2, H.M.S.O.

HOME OFFICE REPORT OF THE WORKING PARTY (1974). Bail Procedures in Magistrates' Courts, H.M.S.O.

KING, M. (1971). *Bail or Custody*, The Cobden Trust, London.

MARTIN, J. P. AND WEBSTER, D. (1971). *Social Consequences of Conviction*, London.

RADZINOWICZ, L. (1957). Ed., *Sexual Offences*, Cambridge Department of Criminal Science, London.

SCOTT, P. D. (1967). Use of remand: bail or custody, in *Royal Commission on the Penal System in England and Wales:* written evidence from government experts, miscellaneous bodies and individual witnesses, **2**, 132–5, H.M.S.O. Reasons for remand in custody, *ibid.*, 147–8.

SELLIN, T. (1958). Recidivism and Maturation, *Natl. Probation and Parole Association J.*, July.

SOOTHILL, K. L. (1974). Repeated medical remands, *Med. Sci. Law*, **14**, 3, 189–99.

SOOTHILL, K. L. AND POPE, P. J. (1974). *Medical Remands in Magistrates' Courts*, Institute for the Study and Treatment of Delinquency, London.

SPARKS, R. F. (1966). The decision to remand for mental exmination, *Brit. J. Criminol.*, **6**, 1, 6–26.

WALKER, N. (1968). *Crime and Insanity in England*, Volume 1, Edinburgh.

WALKER, N. AND MCCABE, S. (1973). *Crime and Insanity in England*, Volume 2, Edinburgh.

WARREN, M. Q. (1969). The case for differential treatment of delinquents, *Annals of Amer. Acad. Politic, Soc. Sci.*, **381**, 45–9, Philadelphia.

WARREN, M. Q. (1973). Correctional treatment in community settings. *International Congress of Criminology*, Madrid.

WEST, D. J. AND BEARCROFT, J. W. (1960). The choice of bail or custody for offenders remanded for a psychiatric report, *Int. J. soc. Psychiat.*, **6**, 34.

ZANDER, M. (1967). Discovering bail applicants' backgrounds, *New Law J.*, August.

ZANDER, M. (1967). Bail: a reappraisal, *Criminal Law Rev.*, January, February, March.

ZANDER, M. (1971). A study of bail/custody decisions in London Magistrates' courts, *Criminal Law Rev.*, April.

INDEX

A. GENERAL REFERENCES

B. STATUTE REFERENCES